HOW TO GO FROM GOOD TO GREAT

Lessons for Management & Leadership
The Key to Growing Your Business

VOL. 1

STEVEN STEWART

TABLE OF CONTENTS

Chapter 1 - Good is the Enemy of Great
Chapter 2 - Level 5 Leadership
Chapter 3 - First Who ... Then What
Chapter 4 - Confront The Brutal Facts (Yet Never Lose Faith)
Chapter 5 - The Hedgehog Concept - (Simplicity within the Three Circles)
Chapter 6 - A Culture of Discipline
Chapter 7 - Technology Accelerators
Chapter 8 - The Flywheel and The Doom Loop
Chapter 9 - From Good To Great To Built To Last
Epilogue - Frequently Asked Questions

Appendix 1.A - Selection Process for Good-To-Great Companies
Appendix 1.B - Direct Comparison Selections
Appendix 1.C - Unsustained Comparisons
Appendix 1.D - Overview of Research Steps
Appendix 2.A - Inside Versus Outside CEO Analysis
Appendix 5.A - Industry Analysis Rankings
Appendix 8.A - Doom Loop Behavior in the Comparison Companies
Appendix 8.B - Summary of Acquisition Analysis

CHAPTER 1
Good is the Enemy of Great

That's what makes death so hard—unsatisfied curiosity.

—BERYL MARKHAM,
West with the Night[1]

Good is the enemy of great.

And that is one of the key reasons why we have so little that becomes great.

We don't have great schools, principally because we have good schools. We don't have great government, principally because we have good government. Few people attain great lives, in large part because it is just so easy to settle for a good life. The vast majority of companies never become great, precisely because the vast majority become quite good—and that is their main problem.

This point became piercingly clear to me in 1996, when I was having dinner with a group of thought leaders gathered for a discussion about organizational performance. Bill Meehan, the managing director of the San Francisco office of McKinsey & Company, leaned over and casually confided, "You know, Jim, we love *Built to Last* around here. You and your coauthor did a very fine job on the research and writing. Unfortunately, it's useless."

Curious, I asked him to explain.

"The companies you wrote about were, for the most part, always great," he said. "They never had to turn themselves from good companies into great companies. They had parents like David Packard and George Merck, who shaped the character of greatness from early on. But what about the vast majority of companies that wake up partway through life and realize that they're good, but not great?"

I now realize that Meehan was exaggerating for effect with his "useless" comment, but his essential observation was correct—that truly great companies, for the most part, have always been great. And the vast majority of good companies remain just that—good, but not great. Indeed, Meehan's comment proved to be an invaluable gift, as it planted the seed of a question that became the basis of this entire book—namely, Can a good company become a great company and, if so, how? Or is the disease of "just being good" incurable?

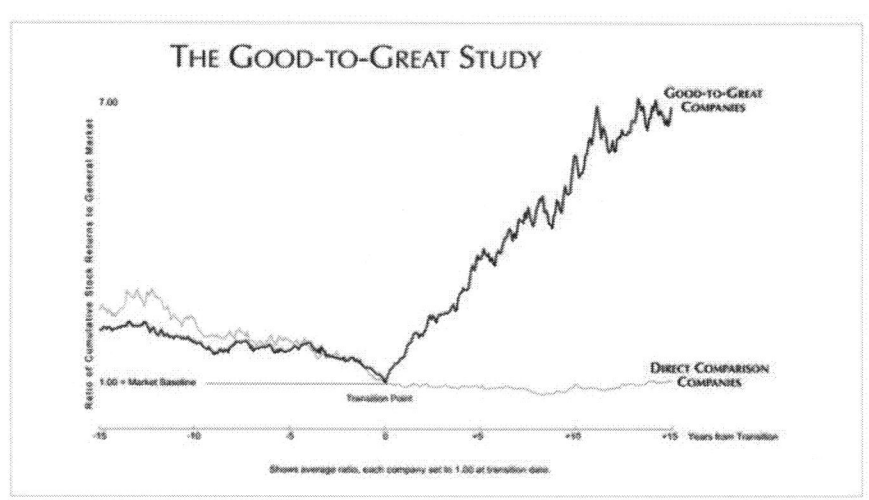

Five years after that fateful dinner we can now say, without question, that good to great *does* happen, and we've learned much about the underlying variables that make it happen. Inspired by Bill Meehan's challenge, my research team and I embarked on a five-year research effort, a journey to explore the inner workings of good to great.

To quickly grasp the concept of the project, look at the chart on page 2.[*] In essence, we identified companies that made the leap from good results to great results and sustained those results for at least fifteen years. We compared these companies to a carefully selected control group of comparison companies that failed to make the leap, or if they did, failed to sustain it. We then compared the good-to-great companies to the comparison companies to discover the essential and distinguishing factors at work.

The good-to-great examples that made the final cut into the study attained extraordinary results, averaging cumulative stock returns 6.9 times the general market in the fifteen years following their transition points.[2] To put that in perspective, General Electric (considered by many to be the best-led company in America at the end of the twentieth century) outperformed the market by 2.8 times over the fifteen years 1985 to 2000.[3] Furthermore, if you invested $1 in a mutual fund of the good-to-great companies in 1965, holding each company at the general market rate until the date of transition, and simultaneously invested $1 in a general market stock fund, your $1 in the good-to-great fund taken out on January 1, 2000, would have multiplied 471 times, compared to a 56 fold increase in the market.[4]

These are remarkable numbers, made all the more remarkable when you consider the fact that they came from companies that had previously been so utterly *un*remarkable. Consider just one case, Walgreens. For over forty years, Walgreens had bumped along as a very average company, more or less tracking the general market. Then in 1975, seemingly out of nowhere—bang!— Walgreens began to climb... and climb...and climb... and climb... and it just kept climbing. From December 31, 1975, to January 1, 2000, $1 invested in Walgreens beat $1 invested in technology superstar Intel by nearly two times, General Electric by nearly five times, Coca-Cola by nearly eight times, and the general stock market (including the NASDAQ stock run-up at the end of 1999) by over *fifteen* times.[*]

Notes:

1. $1 divided evenly across companies in each set, January 1, 1965.
2. Each company held at market rate of return, until transition date.
3. Cumulative value of each fund shown as of January 1, 2000.
4. Dividends reinvested, adjusted for all stock splits.

How on earth did a company with such a long history of being nothing special transform itself into an enterprise that outperformed some of the best-led organizations in the world? And why was Walgreens able to make the leap when other companies in the same industry with the same opportunities and similar resources, such as Eckerd, did *not* make the leap? This single case captures the essence of our quest.

This book is not about Walgreens per se, or any of the specific companies we studied. It is about *the question*—Can a good company become a great company and, if so, how?—and our search for timeless, universal answers that can be applied by any organization.

> Our five-year quest yielded many insights, a number of them surprising and quite contrary to conventional wisdom, but one giant conclusion stands above the others: We believe that almost *any* organization can substantially improve its stature and performance, perhaps even become great, if it conscientiously applies the framework of ideas we've uncovered.

This book is dedicated to teaching what we've learned. The remainder of this introductory chapter tells the story of our journey, outlines our research method, and previews the key findings. In chapter 2, we launch headlong into the findings themselves, beginning with one of the most provocative of the whole study: Level 5 leadership.

UNDAUNTED CURIOSITY

People often ask, "What motivates you to undertake these huge research projects?" It's a good question. The answer is, "Curiosity." There is nothing I find more exciting than picking a question that I don't know the answer to and embarking on a quest for answers. It's deeply satisfying to climb into the boat, like Lewis and Clark, and head west, saying, "We don't know what we'll find when we get there, but we'll be sure to let you know when we get back."

Here is the abbreviated story of this particular odyssey of curiosity.

Phase 1: The Search

With the question in hand, I began to assemble a team of researchers. (When I use "we" throughout this book, I am referring to the research team. In all, twenty-one people worked on the project at key points, usually in teams of four to six at a time.)

Our first task was to find companies that showed the good-to-great pattern exemplified in the chart on page 2. We launched a six-month "death march of financial analysis," looking for companies that showed the following basic pattern: fifteen-year cumulative stock returns at or below the general stock market, punctuated by a transition point, then cumulative returns at least three times the market over the next fifteen years. We picked fifteen years because it would transcend one-hit wonders and lucky breaks (you can't just be lucky for fifteen years) and would exceed the average tenure of most chief executive officers (helping us to separate great companies from companies that just happened to have a single great leader). We picked three times the market because it exceeds the performance of most widely acknowledged great companies. For perspective, a mutual fund of the following "marquis set" of companies beat the market by only 2.5 times over the years 1985 to 2000: 3M, Boeing, Coca-Cola, GE, Hewlett-Packard, Intel, Johnson & Johnson, Merck, Motorola, Pepsi, Procter & Gamble, WalMart, and Walt Disney. Not a bad set to beat.

From an initial universe of companies that appeared on the Fortune 500 in the years 1965 to 1995, we systematically searched and sifted, eventually finding eleven good-to-great examples. (I've put a detailed description of our search in Appendix 1.A.) However, a couple of points deserve brief mention here. First, a company had to demonstrate the good-to-great pattern *independent of its industry*; if the whole industry showed the same pattern, we dropped the company. Second, we debated whether we should use additional selection criteria beyond cumulative stock returns, such as impact on society and employee welfare. We eventually decided to limit our selection to the good-to-great *results* pattern, as we could not conceive of any legitimate and consistent method for selecting on these other variables without introducing our own biases. In the last chapter, however, I address the relationship between corporate values and *enduring* great companies, but the focus of this particular research effort is on the very specific question of how to turn a good organization into one that produces sustained great results.

At first glance, we were surprised by the list. Who would have thought that Fannie Mae would beat companies like GE and Coca-Cola? Or that Walgreens could beat Intel? The surprising list—a dowdier group would be hard to find—taught us a key lesson right up front. It is possible to turn good into great in the most unlikely of situations. This became the first of many surprises that led us to reevaluate our thinking about corporate greatness.

GOOD-TO-GREAT CASES

Company	Results from Transition Point to 15 Years beyond Transition Point*	T Year to T Year + 15
Abbott	3.98 times the market	1974–1989
Circuit City	18.50 times the market	1982–1997
Fannie Mae	7.56 times the market	1984–1999
Gillette	7.39 times the market	1980–1995
Kimberly-Clark	3.42 times the market	1972–1987
Kroger	4.17 times the market	1973–1988
Nucor	5.16 times the market	1975–1990
Philip Morris	7.06 times the market	1964–1979
Pitney Bowes	7.16 times the market	1973–1988
Walgreens	7.34 times the market	1975–1990
Wells Fargo	3.99 times the market	1983–1998

*Ratio of cumulative stock returns relative to the general stock market.

Phase 2: Compared to What?

Next, we took perhaps the most important step in the entire research effort: contrasting the good-to-great companies to a carefully selected set of "comparison companies." The crucial question in our study is *not*, What did the good-to-great companies share in common? Rather, the crucial question is, What did the good-to-great companies share in common that *distinguished* them from the comparison companies? Think of it this way: Suppose you wanted to study what makes gold medal winners in the Olympic Games. If you only studied the gold medal winners by themselves, you'd find that they all had coaches. But if you looked at the athletes that made the Olympic team, but never won a medal, you'd find that they *also* had coaches! The key question is, What systematically *distinguishes* gold medal winners from those who never won a medal?

We selected two sets of comparison companies. The first set consisted of "direct comparisons"—companies that were in the same industry as the good-to-great companies with the same opportunities and similar resources at the time of transition, but that showed no leap from good to great. (See Appendix 1.B for details of our selection process.) The second consisted of "unsustained comparisons"—companies that made a short-term shift from good to great but failed to maintain the trajectory—to address the question of sustainability. (See Appendix 1.C.) In all, this gave us a total study set of twenty-eight companies: eleven good-to-great companies, eleven direct comparisons, and six unsustained comparisons.

THE ENTIRE STUDY SET

Good-to-Great Companies	Direct Comparisons
Abbott	Upjohn
Circuit City	Silo
Fannie Mae	Great Western
Gillette	Warner-Lambert
Kimberly-Clark	Scott Paper
Kroger	A&P
Nucor	Bethlehem Steel
Philip Morris	R. J. Reynolds
Pitney Bowes	Addressograph
Walgreens	Eckerd
Wells Fargo	Bank of America

Unsustained Comparisons

Burroughs
Chrysler
Harris
Hasbro
Rubbermaid
Teledyne

Phase 3: Inside the Black Box

We then turned our attention to a deep analysis of each case. We collected all articles published on the twenty-eight companies, dating back fifty years or more. We systematically coded all the material into categories, such as strategy, technology, leadership, and so forth. Then we interviewed most of the good-to-great executives who held key positions of responsibility during the transition era. We also initiated a wide range of qualitative and quantitative analyses, looking at everything from acquisitions to executive compensation, from business strategy to corporate culture, from layoffs to leadership style, from financial ratios to management turnover. When all was said and done, the total project consumed 10.5 people years of effort. We read and systematically coded nearly 6,000 articles, generated more than 2,000 pages of interview transcripts, and created 384 million bytes of computer data. (See Appendix 1.D for a detailed list of all our analyses and activities.)

We came to think of our research effort as akin to looking inside a black box. Each step along the way was like installing another lightbulb to shed light on the inner workings of the good-to-great process.

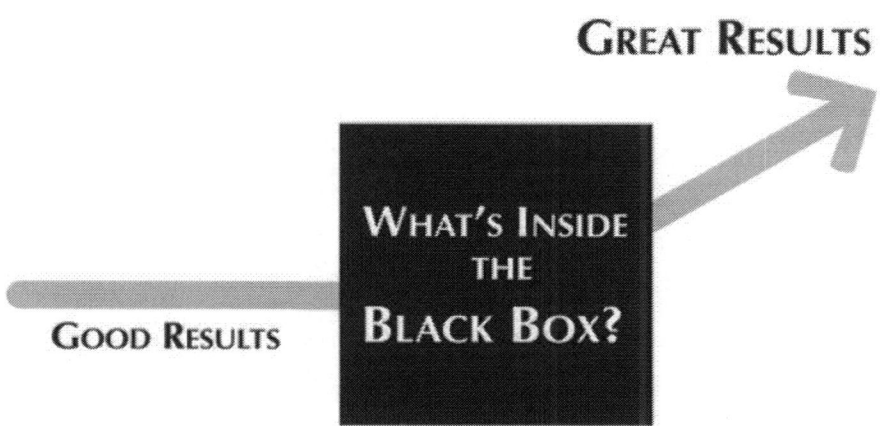

With data in hand, we began a series of weekly research-team debates. For each of the twenty-eight companies, members of the research team and I would systematically read all the articles, analyses, interviews, and the research coding. I would make a presentation to the team on that specific company, drawing potential conclusions and asking questions. Then we would debate, disagree, pound on tables, raise our voices, pause and reflect, debate some more, pause and think, discuss, resolve, question, and debate yet again about "what it all means."

> It is important to understand that we developed all of the concepts in this book by making *empirical* deductions *directly from the data*. We did not begin this project with a theory to test or prove. We sought to build a theory from the ground up, derived directly from the evidence.

The core of our method was a systematic process of contrasting the good-to-great examples to the comparisons, always asking, "What's different?"

We also made particular note of "dogs that did not bark." In the Sherlock

Holmes classic *"The Adventure of Silver Blaze,"* Holmes identified "the curious incident of the dog in the nighttime" as the key clue. It turns out that the dog did nothing in the nighttime and *that*, according to Holmes, was the curious incident, which led him to the conclusion that the prime suspect must have been someone who knew the dog well.

In our study, what we *didn't* find—dogs that we might have expected to bark but didn't—turned out to be some of the best clues to the inner workings of good to great. When we stepped inside the black box and turned on the lightbulbs, we were frequently just as astonished at what we did *not* see as what we did. For example:

- Larger-than-life, celebrity leaders who ride in from the outside are *negatively* correlated with taking a company from good to great. Ten of eleven good-to-great CEOs came from inside the company, whereas the comparison companies tried outside CEOs six times more often.
- We found no systematic pattern linking specific forms of executive compensation to the process of going from good to great. The idea that the structure of executive compensation is a key driver in corporate performance is simply not supported by the data.
- Strategy per se did not separate the good-to-great companies from the comparison companies. Both sets of companies had well-defined strategies, and there is no evidence that the good-to-great companies spent more time on long-range strategic planning than the comparison companies.
- The good-to-great companies did not focus principally on what to *do* to become great; they focused equally on what *not* to do and what to *stop* doing.
- Technology and technology-driven change has virtually nothing to do with igniting a transformation from good to great. Technology can *accelerate* a transformation, but technology cannot *cause* a transformation.
- Mergers and acquisitions play virtually no role in igniting a transformation from good to great; two big mediocrities joined together never make one great company.
- The good-to-great companies paid scant attention to managing change, motivating people, or creating alignment. Under the right conditions, the problems of commitment, alignment, motivation, and change largely melt away.
- The good-to-great companies had no name, tag line, launch event, or

program to signify their transformations. Indeed, some reported being unaware of the magnitude of the transformation at the time; only later, in retrospect, did it become clear. Yes, they produced a truly revolutionary leap in results, but *not* by a revolutionary process.

• The good-to-great companies were not, by and large, in great industries, and some were in terrible industries. In no case do we have a company that just happened to be sitting on the nose cone of a rocket when it took off. Greatness is not a function of circumstance. Greatness, it turns out, is largely a matter of conscious choice.

Phase 4: Chaos to Concept

I've tried to come up with a simple way to convey what was required to go from all the data, analyses, debates, and "dogs that did not bark" to the final findings in this book. The best answer I can give is that it was an iterative process of looping back and forth, developing ideas and testing them against the data, revising the ideas, building a framework, seeing it break under the weight of evidence, and rebuilding it yet again. That process was repeated over and over, until everything hung together in a coherent framework of concepts. We all have a strength or two in life, and I suppose mine is the ability to take a lump of unorganized information, see patterns, and extract order from the mess—to go from chaos to concept.

That said, however, I wish to underscore again that the concepts in the final framework are not my "opinions." While I cannot extract my own psychology and biases entirely from the research, each finding in the final framework met a rigorous standard before the research team would deem it significant. Every primary concept in the final framework showed up as a change variable in 100 percent of the good-to-great companies and in less than 30 percent of the comparison companies during the pivotal years. Any insight that failed this test did not make it into the book as a chapter-level concept.

Here, then, is an overview of the framework of concepts and a preview of what's to come in the rest of the book. (See the diagram below.) Think of the transformation as a process of buildup followed by breakthrough, broken into three broad stages: disciplined people, disciplined thought, and disciplined action. Within each of these three stages, there are two key concepts, shown in the framework and described below. Wrapping around this entire framework is a concept we came to call the flywheel, which captures the gestalt of the entire process of going from good to great.

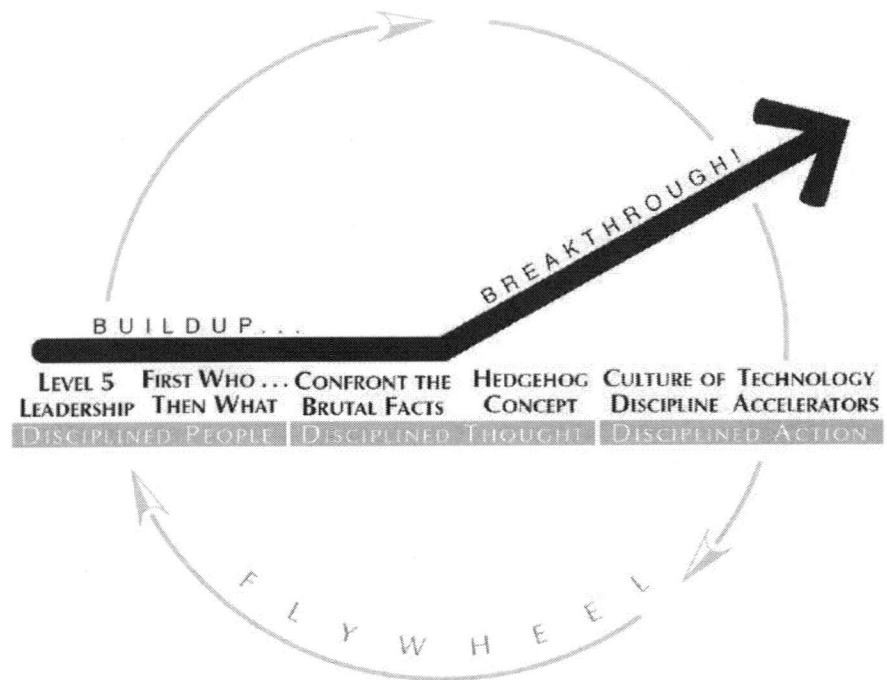

Level 5 Leadership. We were surprised, shocked really, to discover the type of leadership required for turning a good company into a great one. Compared to high-profile leaders with big personalities who make headlines and become celebrities, the good-to-great leaders seem to have come from Mars. Self-effacing, quiet, reserved, even shy—these leaders are a paradoxical blend of personal humility and professional will. They are more like Lincoln and Socrates than Patton or Caesar.

First Who ... Then What. We expected that good-to-great leaders would begin by setting a new vision and strategy. We found instead that they *first* got the right people on the bus, the wrong people off the bus, and the right people in the right seats—and *then* they figured out where to drive it. The old adage "People are your most important asset" turns out to be wrong. People are not your most important asset. The *right* people are.

Confront the Brutal Facts (Yet Never Lose Faith). We learned that a former prisoner of war had more to teach us about what it takes to find a path to greatness than most books on corporate strategy. Every good-to-great company embraced what we came to call the Stockdale Paradox: You must maintain unwavering faith that you can and will prevail in the end, regardless of the difficulties, AND *at the same time* have the discipline to confront the most brutal facts of your current reality, whatever they might be.

The Hedgehog Concept (Simplicity within the Three Circles). To go from good to great requires transcending the curse of competence. Just because something is your core business—just because you've been doing it for years or perhaps even decades—does not necessarily mean you can be the best in the world at it. And if you cannot be the best in the world at your core business, then your core business absolutely cannot form the basis of a great company. It must be replaced with a simple concept that reflects deep understanding of three intersecting circles.

A Culture of Discipline. All companies have a culture, some companies have discipline, but few companies have a *culture of discipline*. When you have disciplined people, you don't need hierarchy. When you have disciplined thought, you don't need bureaucracy. When you have disciplined action, you don't need excessive controls. When you combine a culture of discipline with an ethic of entrepreneurship, you get the magical alchemy of great performance.

Technology Accelerators. Good-to-great companies *think* differently about the role of technology. They never use technology as the primary means of igniting a transformation. Yet, paradoxically, they are pioneers in the application of *carefully selected* technologies. We learned that technology by itself is never a primary, root cause of either greatness or decline.

The Flywheel and the Doom Loop. Those who launch revolutions, dramatic change programs, and wrenching restructurings will almost certainly fail to make the leap from good to great. No matter how dramatic the end result, the good-to-great transformations never happened in one fell swoop. There was no single defining action, no grand program, no one killer innovation, no solitary lucky break, no miracle moment. Rather, the process resembled relentlessly pushing a giant heavy flywheel in one direction, turn upon turn, building momentum until a point of breakthrough, and beyond.

From Good to Great to Built to Last. In an ironic twist, I now see *Good to Great* not as a sequel to *Built to Last,* but as more of a *prequel*. This book is about how to turn a good organization into one that produces sustained great results. *Built to Last* is about how you take a company with great results and turn it into an *enduring* great company of iconic stature. To make that final shift requires core values and a purpose beyond just making money combined with the key dynamic of preserve the core / stimulate progress.

Good to Great Concepts → Sustained Great Results + *Built to Last* Concepts → Enduring Great Company

If you are already a student of *Built to Last*, please set aside your questions about the precise links between the two studies as you embark upon the findings in *Good to Great*. In the last chapter, I return to this question and link the two studies together.

THE TIMELESS "PHYSICS" OF GOOD TO GREAT

I had just finished presenting my research to a set of Internet executives gathered at a conference, when a hand shot up. "Will your findings continue to apply in the new economy? Don't we need to throw out all the old ideas and start from scratch?" It's a legitimate question, as we do live in a time of dramatic change, and it comes up so often that I'd like to dispense with it right up front, before heading into the meat of the book.

Yes, the world is changing, and will continue to do so. But that does not mean we should stop the search for timeless principles. Think of it this way: While the practices of engineering continually evolve and change, the laws of physics remain relatively fixed. I like to think of our work as a search for timeless principles—the enduring physics of great organizations—that will remain true and relevant no matter how the world changes around us. Yes, the specific application will change (the engineering), but certain immutable laws of organized human performance (the physics) will endure.

The truth is, there's nothing new about being in a new economy. Those who faced the invention of electricity, the telephone, the automobile, the radio, or the transistor—did they feel it was any less of a new economy than we feel today? And in each rendition of the new economy, the best leaders have adhered to certain basic principles, with rigor and discipline.

Some people will point out that the scale and pace of change is greater today than anytime in the past. Perhaps. Even so, some of the companies in our good-to-great study faced rates of change that rival anything in the new economy. For example, during the early 1980s, the banking industry was completely transformed in about three years, as the full weight of deregulation came crashing down. It was certainly a new economy for the banking industry! Yet Wells Fargo applied every single finding in this book to produce great results, right smack in the middle of the fast-paced change triggered by deregulation.

> As you immerse yourself in the coming chapters, keep one key point in mind. This book is not about the old economy. Nor is it about the new

economy. It is not even about the companies you're reading about, or even about business per se. It is ultimately about one thing: the timeless principles of good to great. It's about how you take a good organization and turn it into one that produces sustained great results, using whatever definition of results best applies to your organization.

This might come as a surprise, but I don't primarily think of my work as about the study of business, nor do I see this as fundamentally a business book. Rather, I see my work as being about discovering what creates enduring great organizations of *any* type. I'm curious to understand the fundamental differences between great and good, between excellent and mediocre. I just happen to use corporations as a means of getting inside the black box. I do this because publicly traded corporations, unlike other types of organizations, have two huge advantages for research: a widely agreed upon definition of results (so we can rigorously select a study set) and a plethora of easily accessible data.

That good is the enemy of great is not just a business problem. It is a *human* problem. If we have cracked the code on the question of good to great, we should have something of value to any type of organization. Good schools might become great schools. Good newspapers might become great newspapers. Good churches might become great churches. Good government agencies might become great agencies. And good companies might become great companies.

So, I invite you to join me on an intellectual adventure to discover what it takes to turn good into great. I also encourage you to question and challenge what you learn. As one of my favorite professors once said, "The best students are those who never quite believe their professors." True enough. But he also said, "One ought not to reject the data merely because one does not like what the data implies." I offer everything herein for your thoughtful consideration, not blind acceptance. You're the judge and jury. Let the evidence speak.

---

*A description of how the charts on pages 2 and 4 were created appears in chapter 1 notes at the end of the book.

*Calculations of stock returns used throughout this book reflect the total cumulative return to an investor, dividends reinvested and adjusted for stock splits. The "general stock market" (often referred to as simply "the market") reflects the totality of stocks traded on the New York Exchange, American Stock Exchange, and NASDAQ. See the notes to chapter 1 for details on data sources and calculations.

CHAPTER 2
Level 5 Leadership

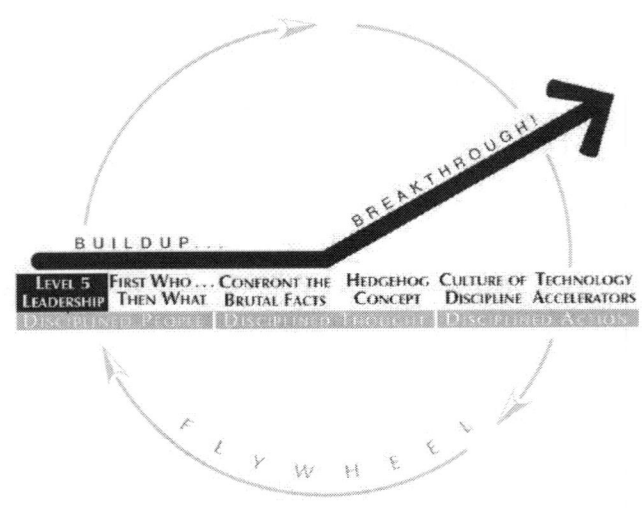

You can accomplish anything in life, provided that you do not mind who gets the credit.

—Harry S. Truman[1]

In 1971, a seemingly ordinary man named Darwin E. Smith became chief executive of Kimberly-Clark, a stodgy old paper company whose stock had fallen 36 percent behind the general market over the previous twenty years.

Smith, the company's mild-mannered in-house lawyer, wasn't so sure the board had made the right choice—a feeling further reinforced when a director pulled Smith aside and reminded him that he lacked some of the qualifications for the position.[2] But CEO he was, and CEO he remained for twenty years.

What a twenty years it was. In that period, Smith created a stunning transformation, turning Kimberly-Clark into the leading paper-based consumer products company in the world. Under his stewardship, Kimberly-Clark generated cumulative stock returns 4.1 times the general market, handily beating its direct rivals Scott Paper and Procter & Gamble and outperforming such venerable companies as Coca-Cola, Hewlett-Packard, 3M, and General Electric.

It was an impressive performance, one of the best examples in the twentieth century of taking a good company and making it great. Yet few people—even ardent students of management and corporate history—know anything about Darwin Smith. He probably would have liked it that way. A man who carried no airs of self-importance, Smith found his favorite companionship among plumbers and electricians and spent his vacations rumbling around his Wisconsin farm in the cab of a backhoe, digging holes and moving rocks.[3] He never cultivated hero status or executive celebrity status.[4] When a journalist asked him to describe his management style, Smith, dressed unfashionably like a farm boy wearing his first suit bought at J. C. Penney, just stared back from the other side of his nerdy-looking black-rimmed glasses. After a long, uncomfortable silence, he said simply: "Eccentric."[5] The *Wall Street Journal* did not write a splashy feature on Darwin Smith.

But if you were to think of Darwin Smith as somehow meek or soft, you would be terribly mistaken. His awkward shyness and lack of pretense was coupled with a fierce, even stoic, resolve toward life. Smith grew up as a poor Indiana farm-town boy, putting himself through college by working the day shift at International Harvester and attending Indiana University at night. One day, he lost part of a finger on the job. The story goes that he went to class that evening and returned to work the next day. While that might be a bit of an exaggeration, he clearly did not let a lost finger slow down his progress toward graduation. He kept working full-time, he kept going to class at night, and he earned admission to Harvard Law School.[6] Later in life, two months after becoming CEO, doctors diagnosed Smith with nose and throat cancer, predicting he had less than a year to live. He informed the board but made it clear that he was not dead yet and had no plans to die anytime soon. Smith held fully to his demanding work schedule while commuting weekly from Wisconsin to Houston for radiation therapy and lived twenty-five more years, most of them as CEO.[7]

Smith brought that same ferocious resolve to rebuilding Kimberly-Clark, especially when he made the most dramatic decision in the company's history: Sell the mills.[8] Shortly after he became CEO, Smith and his team had concluded that the traditional core business—coated paper—was doomed to mediocrity. Its economics were bad and the competition weak.[9] But, they reasoned, if Kimberly-Clark thrust itself into the fire of the *consumer* paper-products industry, world-class competition like Procter & Gamble would force it to achieve greatness or perish.

BEFORE DARWIN SMITH
Kimberly-Clark, Cumulative Value of $1 Invested,
1951 – 1971

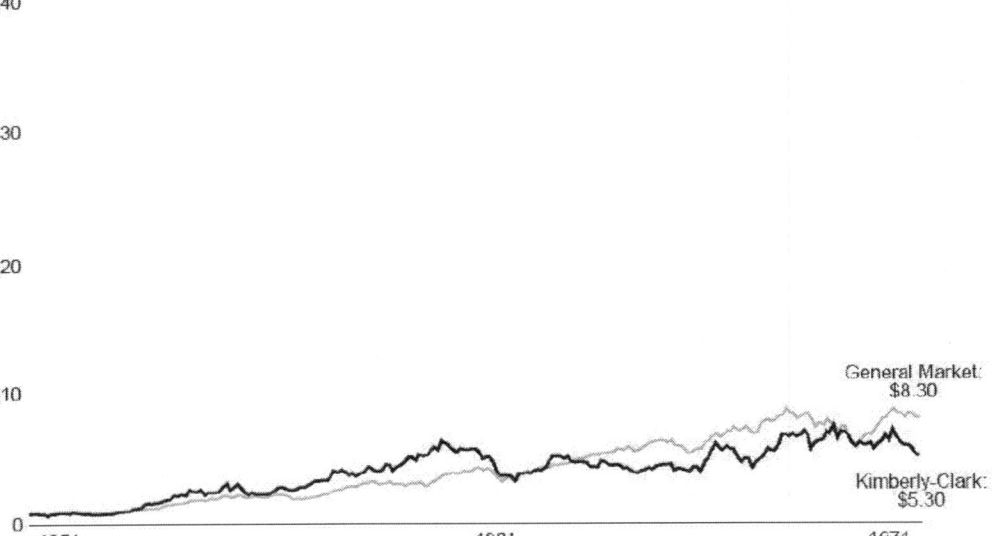

DARWIN SMITH TENURE
Kimberly-Clark, Cumulative Value of $1 Invested,
1971 – 1991

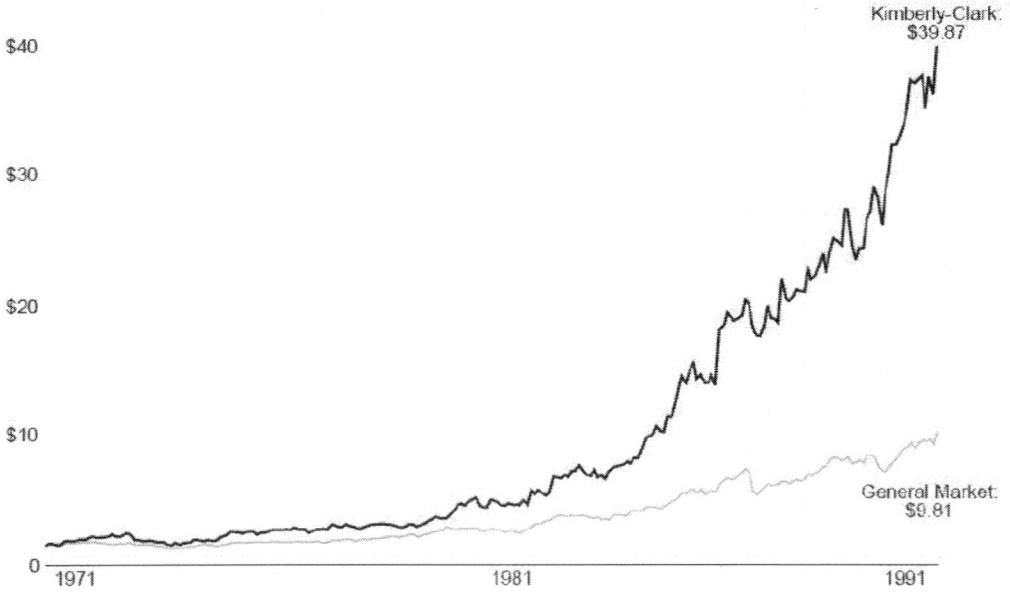

LEVEL 5 **LEVEL 5 EXECUTIVE**
Builds enduring greatness through a paradoxical blend of personal humility and professional will.

LEVEL 4 **EFFECTIVE LEADER**
Catalyzes commitment to and vigorous pursuit of a clear and compelling vision, stimulating higher performance standards.

LEVEL 3 **COMPETENT MANAGER**
Organizes people and resources toward the effective and efficient pursuit of predetermined objectives.

LEVEL 2 **CONTRIBUTING TEAM MEMBER**
Contributes individual capabilities to the achievement of group objectives and works effectively with others in a group setting.

LEVEL 1 **HIGHLY CAPABLE INDIVIDUAL**
Makes productive contributions through talent, knowledge, skills, and good work habits.

LEVEL 5 HIERARCHY

So, like the general who burned the boats upon landing, leaving only one option (succeed or die), Smith announced the decision to sell the mills, in what one board member called the gutsiest move he'd ever seen a CEO make. Sell even the mill in Kimberly, Wisconsin, and throw all the proceeds into the consumer business, investing in brands like Huggies and Kleenex.[10]

The business media called the move stupid and Wall Street analysts downgraded the stock.[11] Smith never wavered. Twenty-five years later, Kimberly-Clark owned Scott Paper outright and beat Procter & Gamble in six of eight product categories.[12] In retirement, Smith reflected on his exceptional performance, saying simply, "I never stopped trying to become qualified for the job."[13]

NOT WHAT WE EXPECTED

Darwin Smith stands as a classic example of what we came to call a Level 5 leader—an individual who blends extreme personal humility with intense professional will. We found leaders of this type at the helm of every good-to-great company during the transition era. Like Smith, they were self-effacing individuals who displayed the fierce resolve to do whatever needed to be done to make the company great.

> Level 5 leaders channel their ego needs away from themselves and into the larger goal of building a great company. It's not that Level 5 leaders have no ego or self-interest. Indeed, they are incredibly ambitious—*but their ambition is first and foremost for the institution, not themselves.*

The term *Level* 5 refers to the highest level in a hierarchy of executive capabilities that we identified in our research. (See the diagram on page 20.) While you don't need to move in sequence from Level 1 to Level 5—it might be possible to fill in some of the lower levels later—fully developed Level 5 leaders embody all five layers of the pyramid. I am not going to belabor all five levels here, as Levels 1 through 4 are somewhat self-explanatory and are discussed extensively by other authors. This chapter will focus instead on the distinguishing traits of the good-to-great leaders—namely level 5 traits—in contrast to the comparison leaders in our study.

But first, please permit a brief digression to set an important context. We were not looking for Level 5 leadership or anything like it. In fact, I gave the research team explicit instructions to *downplay* the role of top executives so that we could avoid the simplistic "credit the leader" or "blame the leader" thinking common today.

To use an analogy, the "Leadership is the answer to everything" perspective is the modern equivalent of the "God is the answer to everything" perspective that held back our scientific understanding of the physical world in the Dark Ages. In the 1500s, people ascribed all events they didn't understand to God. Why did the crops fail? God did it. Why did we have an earthquake? God did it. What holds the planets in place? God. But with the Enlightenment, we began the search for a more scientific understanding—physics, chemistry, biology, and so forth. Not that we became atheists, but we gained deeper understanding about how the universe ticks.

Similarly, every time we attribute everything to "Leadership," we're no different from people in the 1500s. We're simply admitting our ignorance. Not that we should become leadership atheists (leadership *does* matter), but every time we throw our hands up in frustration—reverting back to "Well, the answer must be Leadership!"—we prevent ourselves from gaining deeper, more scientific understanding about what makes great companies tick.

So, early in the project, I kept insisting, "Ignore the executives." But the research team kept pushing back, "No! There is something consistently unusual about them. We can't ignore them." And I'd respond, "But the comparison companies also had leaders, even some great leaders. So, what's different?" Back and forth the debate raged.

Finally—as should always be the case—the data won.

The good-to-great executives were all cut from the same cloth. It didn't matter whether the company was consumer or industrial, in crisis or steady state, offered services or products. It didn't matter when the transition took place or how big the company. All the good-to-great companies had Level 5 leadership at the time of transition. Furthermore, the absence of Level 5 leadership showed up as a consistent pattern in the comparison companies. Given that Level 5 leadership cuts against the grain of conventional wisdom, especially the belief that we need larger-than-life saviors with big personalities to transform companies, it is important to note that Level 5 is an empirical finding, not an ideological one.

HUMILITY + WILL = LEVEL 5

Level 5 leaders are a study in duality: modest and willful, humble and fearless. To quickly grasp this concept, think of United States President Abraham Lincoln (one of the few Level 5 presidents in United States history), who never let his ego get in the way of his primary ambition for the larger cause of an enduring great nation. Yet those who mistook Mr. Lincoln's personal modesty, shy nature, and awkward manner as signs of weakness found themselves terribly mistaken, to the scale of 250,000 Confederate and 360,000 Union lives, including Lincoln's own.[14]

While it might be a bit of a stretch to compare the good-to-great CEOs to Abraham Lincoln, they did display the same duality. Consider the case of

Colman Mockler, CEO of Gillette from 1975 to 1991. During Mockler's tenure, Gillette faced three attacks that threatened to destroy the company's opportunity for greatness. Two attacks came as hostile takeover bids from Revlon, led by Ronald Perelman, a cigar-chomping raider with a reputation for breaking apart companies to pay down junk bonds and finance more hostile raids.[15] The third attack came from Coniston Partners, an investment group that bought 5.9 percent of Gillette stock and initiated a proxy battle to seize control of the board, hoping to sell the company to the highest bidder and pocket a quick gain on their shares.[16] Had Gillette been flipped to Perelman at the price he offered, shareowners would have reaped an instantaneous 44 percent gain on their stock.[17] Looking at a $2.3 billion short-term stock profit across 116 million shares, most executives would have capitulated, pocketing millions from flipping their own stock and cashing in on generous golden parachutes.[18]

Colman Mockler did not capitulate, choosing instead to fight for the future greatness of Gillette, even though he himself would have pocketed a substantial sum on his own shares. A quiet and reserved man, always courteous, Mockler had the reputation of a gracious, almost patrician gentleman. Yet those who mistook Mockler's reserved nature for weakness found themselves beaten in the end. In the proxy fight, senior Gillette executives reached out to thousands of individual investors—person by person, phone call by phone call—and won the battle.

Now, you might be thinking, "But that just sounds like self-serving entrenched management fighting for their interests at the expense of shareholder interests." On the surface, it might look that way, but consider two key facts.

First, Mockler and his team staked the company's future on huge investments in radically new and technologically advanced systems (later known as Sensor and Mach3). Had the takeover been successful, these projects would almost certainly have been curtailed or eliminated, and none of us would be shaving with Sensor, Sensor for Women, or the Mach3—leaving hundreds of millions of people to a more painful daily battle with stubble.[19]

Second, at the time of the takeover battle, Sensor promised significant future profits that were not reflected in the stock price because it was in secret development. With Sensor in mind, the board and Mockler believed that the future value of the shares far exceeded the current price, even with the price premium offered by the raiders. To sell out would have made short-term shareflippers happy but would have been utterly irresponsible to long-term shareholders.

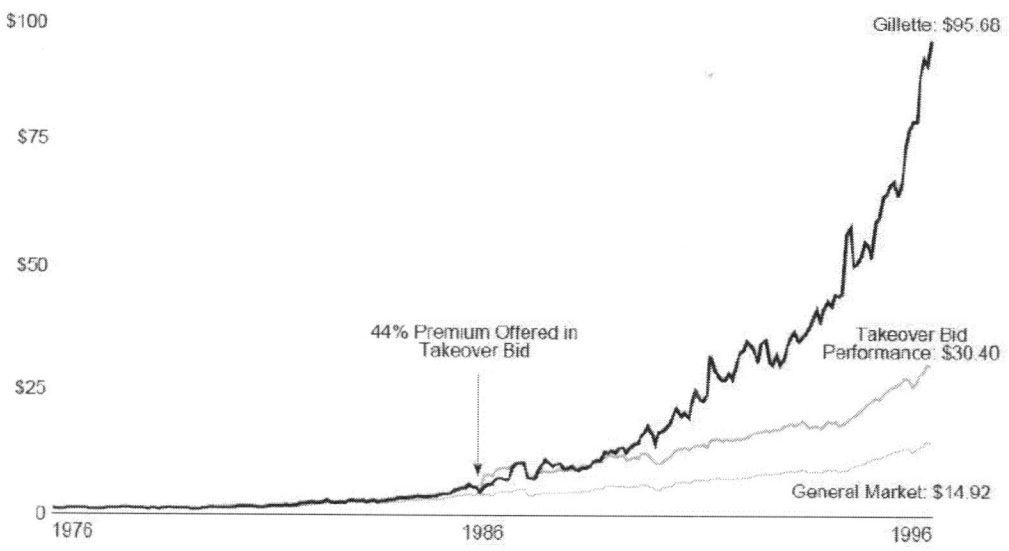

COLMAN MOCKLER'S TRIUMPH
Cumulative Value of $1 Invested, 1976 – 1996
Gillette versus Takeover Bid and Market

This chart shows how an investor would have fared under the following scenarios:

1. $1 invested in Gillette, held from December 31, 1976 through December 31, 1996.

2. $1 invested in Gillette, held from December 31, 1976 *but then sold* to Ronald Perelman for a 44.44% premium on October 31, 1986, the proceeds then invested in the general stock market.

3. $1 invested in General Market held from December 31, 1976 through December 31, 1996.

In the end, Mockler and the board were proved right, stunningly so. If a shareflipper had accepted the 44 percent price premium offered by Ronald Perelman on October 31, 1986, and then invested the full amount in the general market for ten years, through the end of 1996, he would have come out three times *worse* off than a shareholder who had stayed with Mockler and Gillette.[20] Indeed, the company, its customers, *and* the shareholders would have been ill served had Mockler capitulated to the raiders, pocketed his millions, and retired to a life of leisure.

Sadly, Mockler was never able to enjoy the full fruits of his effort. On January 25, 1991, the Gillette team received an advance copy of the cover of *Forbes* magazine, which featured an artist's rendition of Mockler standing atop a mountain holding a giant razor above his head in a triumphal pose, while the vanquished languish on the hillsides below. The other executives razzed the publicity-shy Mockler, who had likely declined requests to be photographed for the cover in the first place, amused at seeing him portrayed as a corporate version of Conan the Triumphant. Walking back to his office, minutes after seeing this public acknowledgment of his sixteen years of struggle, Mockler crumpled to the floor, struck dead by a massive heart attack.[21]

I do not know whether Mockler would have chosen to die in harness, but I am quite confident that he would not have changed his approach as chief executive. His placid persona hid an inner intensity, a dedication to making anything he touched the best it could possibly be—not just because of what he would get, but because he simply couldn't imagine doing it any other way. It wouldn't have been an option within Colman Mockler's value system to take the easy path and turn the company over to those who would milk it like a cow, destroying its potential to become great, any more than it would have been an option for Lincoln to sue for peace and lose forever the chance of an enduring great nation.

Ambition for the Company: Setting Up Successors for Success

When David Maxwell became CEO of Fannie Mae in 1981, the company was losing $1 million every single business day. Over the next nine years, Maxwell transformed Fannie Mae into a high-performance culture that rivaled the best Wall Street firms, earning $4 million every business day and beating the general stock market 3.8 to 1. Maxwell retired while still at the top of his game, feeling that the company would be ill served if he stayed on too long, and turned the company over to an equally capable successor, Jim Johnson. Shortly thereafter, Maxwell's retirement package, which had grown to be worth $20 million based on Fannie Mae's spectacular performance, became a point of controversy in Congress (Fannie Mae operates under a government charter). Maxwell responded by writing a letter to his successor, in which he expressed concern that the controversy would trigger an adverse reaction in Washington that could jeopardize the future of the company. He then instructed Johnson not to pay him the remaining balance—$5.5 million—and asked that the entire amount be contributed to the Fannie Mae foundation for low-income housing.[22]

David Maxwell, like Darwin Smith and Colman Mockler, exemplified a key trait of Level 5 leaders: ambition first and foremost for the company and concern for *its* success rather than for one's own riches and personal renown. Level 5 leaders want to see the company even more successful in the next generation, comfortable with the idea that most people won't even know that the roots of that success trace back to their efforts. As one Level 5 leader said, "I want to look out from my porch at one of the great companies in the world someday and be able to say, 'I used to work there.' "

In contrast, the comparison leaders, concerned more with their own reputation for personal greatness, often failed to set the company up for success in the next generation. After all, what better testament to your own personal greatness than that the place falls apart after you leave?

> In over three quarters of the comparison companies, we found executives who set their successors up for failure or chose weak successors, or both.

Some had the "biggest dog" syndrome—they didn't mind other dogs in the kennel, as long as they remained the biggest one. One comparison CEO was said to have treated successor candidates "the way Henry the VIII treated wives."[23]

Consider the case of Rubbermaid, an unsustained comparison company that grew from obscurity to number one on *Fortune's* annual list of America's Most Admired Companies and then, just as quickly, disintegrated into such sorry shape that it had to be acquired by Newell to save itself. The architect of this remarkable story, a charismatic and brilliant leader named Stanley Gault, became synonymous in the late 1980s with the success of the company. In 312 articles collected on Rubbermaid, Gault comes through as a hard-driving, egocentric executive. In one article, he responds to the accusation of being a tyrant with the statement, "Yes, but I'm a sincere tyrant."[24] In another, drawn directly from his own comments on leading change, the word I appears forty-four times ("I could lead the charge"; "I wrote the twelve objectives"; "I presented and explained the objectives"), whereas the word *we* appears just sixteen times.[25] Gault had every reason to be proud of his executive success. Rubbermaid generated forty consecutive quarters of earnings growth under his leadership—an impressive performance, and one that deserves respect.

But—and this is the key point—Gault did not leave behind a company that would be great without *him*. His chosen successor lasted only one year on the job and the next in line faced a management team so shallow that he had to temporarily shoulder four jobs while scrambling to identify a new number two executive.[26] Gault's successors found themselves struggling not only with a management void, but also with strategic voids that would eventually bring the company to its knees.[27]

Of course, you might say, "Yes, Rubbermaid fell apart after Gault, but that just proves his personal greatness as a leader." Exactly! Gault was indeed a tremendous Level 4 leader, perhaps one of the best in the last fifty years. But he was not a Level 5 leader, and that is one key reason why Rubbermaid went from good to great for a brief shining moment and then, just as quickly, went from great to irrelevant.

A Compelling Modesty

In contrast to the very I-centric style of the comparison leaders, we were struck by how the good-to-great leaders *didn't* talk about themselves. During interviews with the good-to-great leaders, they'd talk about the company and the contributions of other executives as long as we'd like but would deflect discussion about their own contributions. When pressed to talk about themselves, they'd say things like, "I hope I'm not sounding like a big shot." Or, "If the board hadn't picked such great successors, you probably wouldn't be talking with me today." Or, "Did I have a lot to do with it? Oh, that sounds so self-serving. I don't think I can take much credit. We were blessed with marvelous people." Or, "There are plenty of people in this company who could do my job better than I do."

It wasn't just false modesty. Those who worked with or wrote about the good-to-great leaders continually used words like *quiet, humble, modest, reserved, shy, gracious, mild-mannered, self-effacing, understated, did not believe his own clippings*; and so forth. Board member Jim Hlavacek described Ken Iverson, the CEO who oversaw Nucor's transformation from near bankruptcy to one of the most successful steel companies in the world:

> Ken is a very modest and humble man. I've never known a person as successful in doing what he's done that's as modest. And, I work for a lot of CEOs of large companies. And that's true in his private life as well. The simplicity of him. I mean little things like he always gets his dogs at the local pound. He has a simple house that's he's lived in for ages. He only has a carport and he complained to me one day about how he had to use his credit card to scrape the frost off his windows and he broke the credit card. "You know, Ken, there's a solution for it; enclose your carport." And he said, "Ah, heck, it isn't that big of a deal .... " He's that humble and simple.[28]

The eleven good-to-great CEOs are some of the most remarkable CEOs of the century, given that only eleven companies from the Fortune 500 met the exacting standards for entry into this study. Yet, despite their remarkable results, almost no one ever remarked about them! George Cain, Alan Wurtzel, David Maxwell, Colman Mockler, Darwin Smith, Jim Herring, Lyle Everingham, Joe Cullman, Fred Allen, Cork Walgreen, Carl Reichardt—how many of these extraordinary executives had you heard of?

> When we systematically tabulated all 5,979 articles in the study, we found fewer articles surrounding the transition date for the good-to-great companies than for the comparisons, by a factor of two.[29] Furthermore, we rarely found articles that focused on the good-to-great CEOs.

The good-to-great leaders never wanted to become larger-than-life heroes. They never aspired to be put on a pedestal or become unreachable icons. They were seemingly ordinary people quietly producing extraordinary results.

Some of the comparison leaders provide a striking contrast. Scott Paper, the comparison company to Kimberly-Clark, hired a CEO named Al Dunlap, a man cut from a very different cloth than Darwin Smith. Dunlap loudly beat on his own chest, telling anyone who would listen (and many who would prefer not to) about what he had accomplished. Quoted in *Business Week* about his nineteen months atop Scott Paper, he boasted, "The Scott story will go down in the annals of American business history as one of the most successful, quickest turnarounds ever, [making] other turnarounds pale by comparison."[30]

According to *Business Week,* Dunlap personally accrued $100 million for 603 days of work at Scott Paper (that's $165,000 *per day*), largely by slashing the workforce, cutting the R&D budget in half, and putting the company on growth steroids in preparation for sale.[31] After selling off the company and pocketing his quick millions, Dunlap wrote a book about himself, in which he trumpeted his nickname Rambo in Pinstripes. "I love the Rambo movies," he wrote. "Here's a guy who has zero chance of success and always wins. Rambo goes into situations against all odds, expecting to get his brains blown out. But he doesn't. At the end of the day he succeeds, he gets rid of the bad guys. He creates peace out of war. That's what I do, too."[32] Darwin Smith may have enjoyed the mindless Rambo movies as well, but I suspect he never walked out of a theater and said to his wife, "You know, I really relate to this Rambo character; he reminds me of me."

> Granted, the Scott Paper story is one of the more dramatic in our study, but it's not an isolated case. In over two thirds of the comparison cases, we noted the presence of a gargantuan personal ego that contributed to the demise or continued mediocrity of the company.[33]

We found this pattern particularly strong in the unsustained comparisons—cases where the company would show a leap in performance under a talented yet egocentric leader, only to decline in later years. Lee Iacocca, for example, saved Chrysler from the brink of catastrophe, performing one of the most celebrated (and deservedly so) turnarounds in American business history. Chrysler rose to a height of 2.9 times the market at a point about halfway through his tenure. Then, however, he diverted his attention to making himself one of the most celebrated CEOs in American business history. *Investor's Business Daily* and the *Wall Street Journal* chronicled how Iacocca appeared regularly on talk shows like the *Today* show and *Larry King Live*, personally starred in over eighty commercials, entertained the idea of running for president of the United States (quoted at one point, "Running Chrysler has been a bigger job than running the country....I could handle the national economy in six months"), and widely promoted his autobiography. The book, *Iacocca*, sold seven million copies and elevated him to rock star status, leading him to be mobbed by thousands of cheering fans upon his arrival in Japan.[34] Iacocca's personal stock soared, but in the second half of his tenure, Chrysler's stock fell 31 percent behind the general market.

Sadly, Iacocca had trouble leaving center stage and letting go of the perks of executive kingship. He postponed his retirement so many times that insiders at Chrysler began to joke that Iacocca stood for "I Am Chairman of Chrysler Corporation Always."[35] And when he did finally retire, he demanded that the board continue to provide a private jet and stock options.[36] Later, he joined forces with noted takeover artist Kirk Kerkorian to launch a hostile takeover bid for Chrysler.[37]

Chrysler experienced a brief return to glory in the five years after Iacocca's retirement, but the company's underlying weaknesses eventually led to a buyout by German carmaker Daimler-Benz.[38] Certainly, the demise of Chrysler as a stand-alone company does not rest entirely on Iacocca's shoulders (the next generation of management made the fateful decision to sell the company to the

Germans), but the fact remains: Iacocca's brilliant turnaround in the early 1980s did not prove to be sustained and Chrysler failed to become an enduring great company.

Unwavering Resolve ... to Do What Must Be Done

It is very important to grasp that Level 5 leadership is not just about humility and modesty. It is equally about ferocious resolve, an almost stoic determination to do whatever needs to be done to make the company great.

Indeed, we debated for a long time on the research team about how to describe the good-to-great leaders. Initially, we penciled in terms like "selfless executive" and "servant leader." But members of the team violently objected to these characterizations.

"Those labels don't ring true," said Anthony Chirikos. "It makes them sound weak or meek, but that's not at all the way I think of Darwin Smith or Colman Mockler. They would do almost anything to make the company great."

Then Eve Li suggested, "Why don't we just call them Level 5 leaders? If we put a label like 'selfless' or 'servant' on them, people will get entirely the wrong idea. We need to get people to engage with the whole concept, to see *both* sides of the coin. If you only get the humility side, you miss the whole idea."

Level 5 leaders are fanatically driven, infected with an incurable need to produce *results*. They will sell the mills or fire their brother, if that's what it takes to make the company great.

When George Cain became CEO of Abbott Laboratories, it sat in the bottom quartile of the pharmaceutical industry, a drowsy enterprise that had lived for years off its cash cow, erythromycin. Cain didn't have an inspiring personality to galvanize the company, but he had something much more powerful: inspired standards. He could not stand mediocrity in any form and was utterly intolerant of anyone who would accept the idea that good is good enough. Cain then set out to destroy one of the key causes of Abbott's mediocrity: nepotism. Systematically rebuilding both the board and the executive team with the best people he could find, Cain made it clear that neither family ties nor length of tenure would have anything to do with whether you held a key position in the company. If you didn't have the capacity to become the best executive in the industry in your span of responsibility, then you would lose your paycheck.[39]

Such rigorous rebuilding might be expected from an outsider brought in to turn the company around, but Cain was an eighteen-year veteran insider *and* a family member, the son of a previous Abbott president. Holiday gatherings were probably tense for a few years in the Cain clan. ("Sorry I had to fire you. Want another slice of turkey?") In the end, though, family members were quite pleased with the performance of their stock, for Cain set in motion a profitable growth machine that, from its transition date in 1974 to 2000, created shareholder returns that beat the market 4.5 to 1, handily outperforming industry superstars Merck and Pfizer.

Upjohn, the direct comparison company to Abbott, also had family leadership during the same era as George Cain. Unlike George Cain, Upjohn's CEO never showed the same resolve to break the mediocrity of nepotism. By the time Abbott had filled all key seats with the best people, regardless of family background, Upjohn still had B level family members holding key positions.[40] Virtually identical companies with identical stock charts up to the point of transition, Upjohn then fell 89 percent behind Abbott over the next twenty-one years before capitulating in a merger to Pharmacia in 1995.

As an interesting aside, Darwin Smith, Colman Mockler, and George Cain came from inside the company. Stanley Gault, Al Dunlap, and Lee Iacocca rode in as saviors from the outside, trumpets blaring. This reflects a more systematic finding from our study. The evidence does not support the idea that you need an outside leader to come in and shake up the place to go from good to great. In fact, going for a high-profile outside change agent is *negatively correlated* with a sustained transformation from good to great. (See Appendix 2.A.)

> Ten out of eleven good-to-great CEOs came from *inside* the company, three of them by family inheritance. The comparison companies turned to outsiders with *six times* greater frequency—yet they failed to produce sustained great results.[41]

A superb example of insider-driven change comes from Charles R. "Cork" Walgreen 3d, who transformed dowdy Walgreens into a company that outperformed the stock market by over fifteen times from the end of 1975 to January 1, 2000.[42] After years of dialogue and debate within his executive team about Walgreens' food-service operations, Cork sensed that the team had finally reached a watershed point of clarity and understanding: Walgreens' brightest future lay in convenient drugstores, not food service. Dan Jorndt, who succeeded Walgreen as CEO in 1998, described what happened next:

Cork said at one of our planning committee meetings, "Okay, now I am going to draw the line in the sand. We are going to be out of the restaurant business completely in five years." At the time, we had over five hundred restaurants. You could have heard a pin drop. He said, "I want to let everybody know the clock is ticking .... " Six months later, we were at our next planning committee meeting and someone mentioned just in passing that we only had five years to be out of the restaurant business. Cork was not a real vociferous fellow. He sort of tapped on the table and said, "Listen, you have four and a half years. I said you had five years six months ago. Now you've got four and a half years." Well, that next day, things really clicked into gear to winding down our restaurant business. He never wavered. He never doubted; he never second-guessed.[43]

Like Darwin Smith selling the mills at Kimberly-Clark, Cork Walgreen's decision required stoic resolve. Not that food service was the largest part of the business (although it did add substantial profits to the bottom line). The real problem was more emotional. Walgreens had, after all, invented the malted milkshake and food service was a long-standing family tradition dating back to his grandfather. Some food-service outlets were even named after the CEO himself—a restaurant chain named Corky's. But no matter, if Walgreens had to fly in the face of long-standing family tradition in order to focus its resources where it could be the best in the world (convenient drugstores), Cork would do it. Quietly, doggedly, simply.[44]

The quiet, dogged nature of Level 5 leaders showed up not only in big decisions, like selling off the food-service operations or fighting corporate raiders, but also in a personal style of sheer workmanlike diligence. Alan Wurtzel, a second-generation family member who took over his family's small company and turned it into Circuit City, perfectly captured the gestalt of this trait. When asked about differences between himself and his counterpart CEO at Circuit City's comparison company, Wurtzel summed up: "The show horse and the plow horse—he was more of a show horse, whereas I was more of a plow horse."[45]

The Window and the Mirror

Alan Wurtzel's plow horse comment is fascinating in light of two other facts. First, he holds a doctor of jurisprudence degree from Yale—clearly, his plow horse nature had nothing to do with a lack of intelligence. Second, his plow horse approach set the stage for truly *best in show* results. Let me put it this way: If you had to choose between $1 invested in Circuit City or $1 invested in General Electric on the day that the legendary Jack Welch took over GE in 1981 and held to January 1, 2000, you would have been better off with Circuit City—by six times.[46] Not a bad performance, for a plow horse.

You might expect that extraordinary results like these would lead Alan Wurtzel to discuss the brilliant decisions he made. But when we asked him to list the top five factors in his company's transformation, ranked by importance, Wurtzel gave a surprising answer: The number one factor was *luck*. "We were in a great industry, with the wind at our backs."

We pushed back, pointing out that we selected the good-to-great companies based on performance that surpassed their industry's average. Furthermore, the comparison company (Silo) was in the same industry, with the same wind and probably bigger sails! We debated the point for a few minutes, with Wurtzel continuing his preference for attributing much of his success to just being in the right place at the right time. Later, when asked to discuss the factors behind the enduring nature of the transformation, he said, "The first thing that comes to mind is luck....I was lucky to find the right successor."[47]

Luck. What an odd factor to talk about. Yet the good-to-great executives talked a lot about luck in our interviews. In one interview with a Nucor executive, we asked why the company had such a remarkable track record of good decisions; he responded: "I guess we were just lucky."[48] Joseph F. Cullman 3d, the Level 5 transition CEO of Philip Morris, flat-out refused to take credit for his company's success, attributing his good fortune to having great colleagues, successors, and predecessors.[49] Even the book he wrote—a book he undertook at the urging of his colleagues, which he never intended to distribute widely outside the company—had the unusual title *I'm a Lucky Guy*. The opening paragraph reads: "I was a very lucky guy from the very beginning of my life: marvelous parents, good genes, lucky in love, lucky in business, and lucky when a Yale classmate had my orders changed to report to Washington, D.C., in early 1941, instead of to a ship that was sunk with all hands lost in the North Atlantic, lucky to be in the Navy, and lucky to be alive at eighty-five."[50]

We were at first puzzled by this emphasis on good luck. After all, we found no evidence that the good-to-great companies were blessed with more good luck (or more bad luck, for that matter) than the comparison companies. Then we began to notice a contrasting pattern in the comparison executives: They credited substantial blame to *bad* luck, frequently bemoaning the difficulties of the environment they faced.

Compare Bethlehem Steel to Nucor. Both companies operated in the steel industry and produced hard-to-differentiate products. Both companies faced the competitive challenge of cheap imported steel. Yet executives at the two companies had completely different views of the same environment. Bethlehem Steel's CEO summed up the company's problems in 1983 by blaming imports: "Our first, second, and third problems are imports."[51] Ken Iverson and his crew at Nucor considered the same challenge from imports a *blessing*, a stroke of good fortune ("Aren't we lucky; steel is heavy, and they have to ship it all the way across the ocean, giving us a huge advantage!"). Iverson saw the first, second, and third problems facing the American steel industry not to be imports, but *management*.[52] He even went so far as to speak out publicly against government protection against imports, telling a stunned gathering of fellow steel executives in 1977 that the real problems facing the American steel industry lay in the fact that management had failed to keep pace with innovation.[53]

The emphasis on luck turns out to be part of a pattern that we came to call *the window and the mirror*.

> Level 5 leaders look out the window to apportion credit to factors outside themselves when things go well (and if they cannot find a specific person or event to give credit to, they credit good luck). At the same time, they look in the mirror to apportion responsibility, never blaming bad luck when things go poorly.

The comparison leaders did just the opposite. They'd look out the window for something or someone outside themselves to blame for poor results, but would preen in front of the mirror and credit themselves when things went well. Strangely, the window and the mirror do not reflect objective reality. Everyone outside the window points inside, directly at the Level 5 leader, saying, "He was the key; without his guidance and leadership, we would not have become a great company." And the Level 5 leader points right back out the window and says, "Look at all the great people and good fortune that made this possible; I'm a lucky guy." They're both right, of course. But the Level 5s would never admit that fact.

CULTIVATING LEVEL 5 LEADERSHIP

Not long ago, I shared the Level 5 finding with a gathering of senior executives. A woman who had recently become chief executive of her company raised her hand and said, "I believe what you say about the good-to-great leaders. But I'm disturbed because when I look in the mirror, I know that I'm not Level 5, not yet anyway. Part of the reason I got this job is because of my ego drives. Are you telling me that I can't make this a great company if I'm not Level 5?"

"I don't know for certain that you absolutely must be a Level 5 leader to make your company great," I replied. "I will simply point back to the data: Of 1,435 companies that appeared on the Fortune 500 in our initial candidate list, only eleven made the very tough cut into our study. In those eleven, all of them had Level 5 leadership in key positions, including the CEO, at the pivotal time of transition."

She sat there, quiet for moment, and you could tell everyone in the room was mentally urging her to ask *the question*. Finally, she said, "Can you learn to become Level 5?"

Summary: The Two Sides of Level 5 Leadership

Professional Will

Creates superb results, a clear catalyst in the transition from good to great.

Demonstrates an unwavering resolve to do whatever must be done to produce the best long-term results, no matter how difficult.

Sets the standard of building an enduring great company; will settle for nothing less.

Looks in the mirror, not out the window, to apportion responsibility for poor results, never blaming other people, external factors, or bad luck.

Personal Humility

Demonstrates a compelling modesty, shunning public adulation; never boastful.

Acts with quiet, calm determination; relies principally on inspired standards, not inspiring charisma, to motivate.

Channels ambition into the company, not the self; sets up successors for even greater success in the next generation.

Looks out the window, not in the mirror, to apportion credit for the success of the company—to other people, external factors, and good luck.

My hypothesis is that there are two categories of people: those who do not have the seed of Level 5 and those who do. The first category consists of people who could never in a million years bring themselves to subjugate their egoistic needs to the greater ambition of building something larger and more lasting than themselves. For these people, work will always be first and foremost about what they *get*—fame, fortune, adulation, power, whatever—not what they *build*, create, and contribute.

The great irony is that the animus and personal ambition that often drive people to positions of power stand at odds with the humility required for Level 5 leadership. When you combine that irony with the fact that boards of directors frequently operate under the false belief that they need to hire a larger-than-life, egocentric leader to make an organization great, you can quickly see why Level 5 leaders rarely appear at the top of our institutions.

The second category of people—and I suspect the larger group—consists of those who have the potential to evolve to Level 5; the capability resides within them, perhaps buried or ignored, but there nonetheless. And under the right circumstances—self-reflection, conscious personal development, a mentor, a great teacher, loving parents, a significant life experience, a Level 5 boss, or any number of other factors—they begin to develop.

In looking at the data, we noticed that some of the leaders in our study had significant life experiences that might have sparked or furthered their maturation. Darwin Smith fully blossomed after his experience with cancer. Joe Cullman was profoundly affected by his World War II experiences, particularly the last-minute change of orders that took him off a doomed ship on which he surely would have died.[54] A strong religious belief or conversion might also nurture development of Level 5 traits. Colman Mockler, for example, converted to evangelical Christianity while getting his MBA at Harvard, and later, according to the book *Cutting Edge*, became a prime mover in a group of Boston business executives who met frequently over breakfast to discuss the carryover of religious values to corporate life.[55] Other leaders in our study, however, had no obvious catalytic event; they just led normal lives and somehow ended up atop the Level 5 hierarchy.

I believe—although I cannot prove—that potential Level 5 leaders are highly prevalent in our society. *The problem is not, in my estimation, a dearth of potential Level 5 leaders. They exist all around us, if we just know what to look for.* And what is that? Look for situations where extraordinary results exist but where no individual steps forth to claim excess credit. You will likely find a potential Level 5 leader at work.

For your own development, I would love to be able to give you a list of steps for becoming Level 5, but we have no solid research data that would support a credible list. Our research exposed Level 5 as a key component inside the black box of what it takes to shift a *company* from good to great. Yet inside that black box is yet another black box—namely, the inner development of a *person to*

Level 5. We could speculate on what might be inside that inner black box, but it would mostly be just that—speculation. So, in short, Level 5 is a very satisfying idea, a powerful idea, and, to produce the best transitions from good to great, perhaps an essential idea. A "Ten-Step List to Level 5" would trivialize the concept.

My best advice, based on the research, is to begin practicing the other good-to-great disciplines we discovered. We found a symbiotic relationship between Level 5 and the remaining findings. On the one hand, Level 5 traits enable you to implement the other findings; on the other hand, practicing the other findings helps you to become Level 5. Think of it this way: This chapter is about what Level 5s *are*; the rest of the book describes what they *do*. Leading with the other disciplines can help you move in the right direction. There is no guarantee that doing so will turn you into a full-fledged Level 5, but it gives you a tangible place to begin.

We cannot say for sure what percentage of people have the seed within, or how many of those can nurture it. Even those of us who discovered Level 5 on the research team do not know for ourselves whether we will succeed in fully evolving to Level 5. And yet, all of us who worked on the finding have been deeply affected and inspired by the idea. Darwin Smith, Colman Mockler, Alan Wurtzel, and all the other Level 5s we learned about have become models for us, something worthy to aspire toward. Whether or not we make it all the way to Level 5, it is worth the effort. For like all basic truths about what is best in human beings, when we catch a glimpse of that truth, we know that our own lives and all that we touch will be the better for the effort.

Chapter Summary
Level 5 Leadership

KEY POINTS

- Every good-to-great company had Level 5 leadership during the pivotal transition years.

- "Level 5" refers to a five-level hierarchy of executive capabilities, with Level 5 at the top. Level 5 leaders embody a paradoxical mix of personal humility and professional will. They are ambitious, to be sure, but ambitious first and foremost for the company, not themselves.

- Level 5 leaders set up their successors for even greater success in the next generation, whereas egocentric Level 4 leaders often set up their successors for failure.

- Level 5 leaders display a compelling modesty, are self-effacing and understated. In contrast, two thirds of the comparison companies had leaders with gargantuan personal egos that contributed to the demise or continued mediocrity of the company.

- Level 5 leaders are fanatically driven, infected with an incurable need to produce sustained *results*. They are resolved to do whatever it takes to make the company great, no matter how big or hard the decisions.

- Level 5 leaders display a workmanlike diligence—more plow horse than show horse.

- Level 5 leaders look out the window to attribute success to factors other than themselves. When things go poorly, however, they look in the mirror and blame themselves, taking full responsibility. The comparison CEOs often did just the opposite—they looked in the mirror to take credit for success, but out the window to assign blame for disappointing results.

- One of the most damaging trends in recent history is the tendency (especially by boards of directors) to select dazzling, celebrity leaders and to de-select potential Level 5 leaders.

• I believe that potential Level 5 leaders exist all around us, if we just know what to look for, and that many people have the potential to evolve into Level 5.

UNEXPECTED FINDINGS

• Larger-than-life, celebrity leaders who ride in from the outside are negatively correlated with going from good to great. Ten of eleven good-to-great CEOs came from *inside* the company, whereas the comparison companies tried outside CEOs six times more often.

• Level 5 leaders attribute much of their success to good luck, rather than personal greatness.

• We were not looking for Level 5 leadership in our research, or anything like it, but the data was overwhelming and convincing. It is an empirical, not an ideological, finding.

CHAPTER 2
First Who...Then What

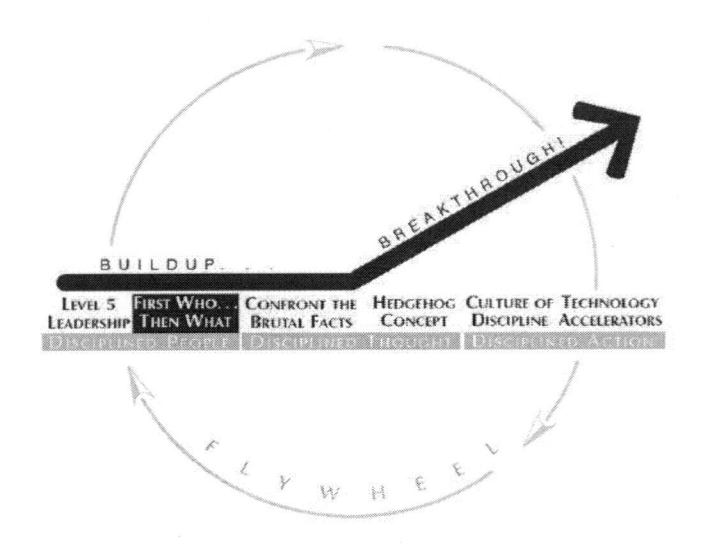

> There are going to be times when we can't wait for somebody. Now, you're either on the bus or off the bus.
>
> —Ken Kesey,
> from *The Electric Kool-Aid Acid Test* by Tom Wolfe[1]

When we began the research project, we expected to find that the first step in taking a company from good to great would be to set a new direction, a new vision and strategy for the company, and then to get people committed and aligned behind that new direction.

We found something quite the opposite.

The executives who ignited the transformations from good to great did not first figure out where to drive the bus and then get people to take it there. No, they *first* got the right people on the bus (and the wrong people off the bus) and *then* figured out where to drive it. They said, in essence, "Look, I don't really know where we should take this bus. But I know this much: If we get the right people on the bus, the right people in the right seats, and the wrong people off the bus, then we'll figure out how to take it someplace great."

The good-to-great leaders understood three simple truths. First, if you begin with "who," rather than "what," you can more easily adapt to a changing world. If people join the bus primarily because of where it is going, what happens if you get ten miles down the road and you need to change direction? You've got a problem. But if people are on the bus because of who else is on the bus, then it's much easier to change direction: "Hey, I got on this bus because of who else is on it; if we need to change direction to be more successful, fine with me." Second, if you have the right people on the bus, the problem of how to motivate and manage people largely goes away. The right people don't need to be tightly managed or fired up; they will be self-motivated by the inner drive to produce the best results and to be part of creating something great. Third, if you have the wrong people, it doesn't matter whether you discover the right direction; you *still* won't have a great company. Great vision without great people is irrelevant.

Consider the case of Wells Fargo. Wells Fargo began its fifteen-year stint of spectacular performance in 1983, but the foundation for the shift dates back to the early 1970s, when then-CEO Dick Cooley began building one of the most talented management teams in the industry (*the* best team, according to investor Warren Buffett).[2] Cooley foresaw that the banking industry would eventually undergo wrenching change, but he did not pretend to know what form that change would take. So instead of mapping out a strategy for change, he and chairman Ernie Arbuckle focused on "injecting an endless stream of talent" directly into the veins of the company. They hired outstanding people whenever and wherever they found them, often without any specific job in mind. "That's how you build the future," he said. "If I'm not smart enough to see the changes that are coming, they will. And they'll be flexible enough to deal with them."[3]

Cooley's approach proved prescient. No one could predict all the changes that would be wrought by banking deregulation. Yet when these changes came, no bank handled those challenges better than Wells Fargo. At a time when its sector of the banking industry fell 59 percent behind the general stock market, Wells Fargo outperformed the market by over three times.[4]

Carl Reichardt, who became CEO in 1983, attributed the bank's success largely to the people around him, most of whom he inherited from Cooley.[5] As he listed members of the Wells Fargo executive team that had joined the company during the Cooley-Reichardt era, we were stunned. Nearly every person had gone on to become CEO of a major company: Bill Aldinger became the CEO of Household Finance, Jack Grundhofer became CEO of U.S. Bancorp,

Frank Newman became CEO of Bankers Trust, Richard Rosenberg became CEO of Bank of America, Bob Joss became CEO of Westpac Banking (one of the largest banks in Australia) and later became dean of the Graduate School of Business at Stanford University—not exactly your garden variety executive team! Arjay Miller, an active Wells Fargo board member for seventeen years, told us that the Wells Fargo team reminded him of the famed "Whiz Kids" recruited to Ford Motor Company in the late 1940s (of which Miller was a member, eventually becoming president of Ford).[6] Wells Fargo's approach was simple: You get the best people, you build them into the best managers in the industry, and you accept the fact that some of them will be recruited to become CEOs of other companies.[7]

Bank of America took a very different approach. While Dick Cooley systematically recruited the best people he could get his hands on, Bank of America, according to the book *Breaking the Bank*, followed something called the "weak generals, strong lieutenants" model.[8] If you pick strong generals for key positions, their competitors will leave. But if you pick weak generals— placeholders, rather than highly capable executives— then the strong lieutenants are more likely to stick around.

The weak generals model produced a climate very different at Bank of America than the one at Wells Fargo. Whereas the Wells Fargo crew acted as a strong team of equal partners, ferociously debating eyeball-to-eyeball in search of the best answers, the Bank of America weak generals would wait for directions from above. Sam Armacost, who inherited the weak generals model, described the management climate: "I came away quite distressed from my first couple of management meetings. Not only couldn't I get conflict, I couldn't even get comment. They were all waiting to see which way the wind blew."[9]

A retired Bank of America executive described senior managers in the 1970s as "Plastic People" who'd been trained to quietly submit to the dictates of a domineering CEO.[10] Later, after losing over $1 billion in the mid-1980s, Bank of America recruited a gang of strong generals to turn the bank around. And where did it find those strong generals? From right across the street at Wells Fargo. In fact, Bank of America recruited so many Wells Fargo executives during its turnaround that people inside began to refer to themselves as "Wells of America."[11] At that point, Bank of America began to climb upward again, but it was too little too late. From 1973 to 1998, while Wells Fargo went from buildup to breakthrough results, Bank of America's cumulative stock returns didn't even keep pace with the general market.

WELLS FARGO VERSUS BANK OF AMERICA
Cumulative Value of $1 Invested,
January 1, 1973 – January 1, 1998

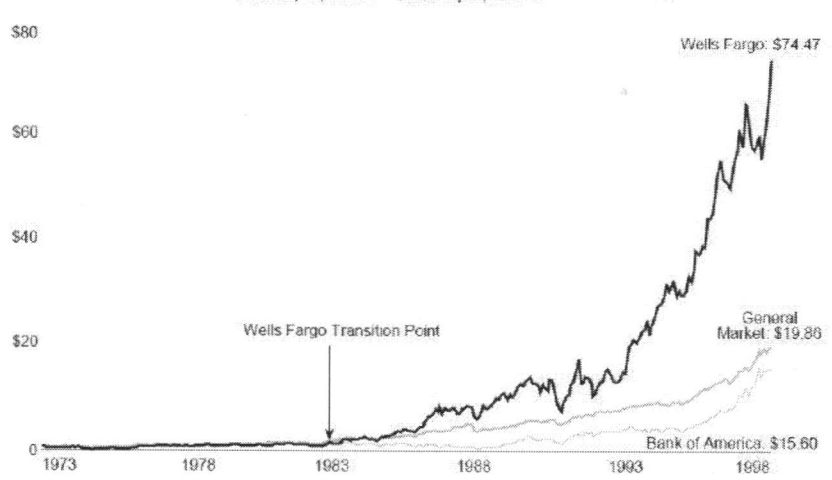

[Chart showing Wells Fargo: $74.47, General Market: $19.86, Bank of America: $15.60, with Wells Fargo Transition Point marked around 1983]

Now, you might be thinking, "That's just good management—the idea of getting the right people around you. What's new about that?" On one level, we have to agree; it is just plain old-fashioned good management. But what stands out with such distinction in the good-to-great companies are two key points that made them quite different.

To be clear, the main point of this chapter is not just about assembling the right team—that's nothing new. The main point is to *first* get the right people on the bus (and the wrong people off the bus) *before* you figure out where to drive it. The second key point is the degree of *sheer rigor* needed in people decisions in order to take a company from good to great.

"First who" is a very simple idea to grasp, and a very difficult idea to *do*—and most don't do it well. It's easy to *talk about* paying attention to people decisions, but how many executives have the discipline of David Maxwell, who held off on developing a strategy until he got the right people in place, *while the company was losing $1 million every single business day* with $56 billion of loans underwater? When Maxwell became CEO of Fannie Mae during its darkest days, the board desperately wanted to know how he was going to rescue the company. Despite the immense pressure to act, to do something dramatic, to seize the wheel and start driving, Maxwell focused first on getting the right people on the Fannie Mae management team. His first act was to interview all the officers. He sat them down and said, "Look, this is going to be a very hard challenge. I want you to think about how demanding this is going to be. If you don't think you're going to like it, that's fine. Nobody's going to hate you."[12]

Maxwell made it absolutely clear that there would only be seats for A players who were going to put forth an A+ effort, and if you weren't up for it, you had better get off the bus, and get off now.[13] One executive who had just uprooted his life and career to join Fannie Mae came to Maxwell and said, "I listened to you very carefully, and I don't want to do this." He left and went back to where he came from.[14] In all, fourteen of twenty-six executives left the company, replaced by some of the best, smartest, and hardest-working executives in the entire world of finance.[15] The same standard applied up and down the Fannie Mae ranks as managers at every level increased the caliber of their teams and put immense peer pressure upon each other, creating high turnover at first, when some people just didn't pan out.[16] "We had a saying, 'You can't fake it at Fannie Mae,' " said one executive team member. "Either you knew your stuff or you didn't, and if you didn't, you'd just blow out of here."[17]

Wells Fargo and Fannie Mae both illustrate the idea that "who" questions come before "what" questions—before vision, before strategy, before tactics, before organizational structure, before technology. Dick Cooley and David Maxwell both exemplified a classic Level 5 style when they said, "I don't know where we should take this company, but I do know that if I start with the right people, ask them the right questions, and engage them in vigorous debate, we will find a way to make this company great."

NOT A "GENIUS WITH A THOUSAND HELPERS"

In contrast to the good-to-great companies, which built deep and strong executive teams, many of the comparison companies followed a "genius with a thousand helpers" model. In this model, the company is a platform for the talents of an extraordinary individual. In these cases, the towering genius, the primary driving force in the company's success, is a great asset— as long as the genius sticks around. The geniuses seldom build great management teams, for the simple reason that they don't need one, and often don't want one. If you're a genius, you don't need a Wells Fargo–caliber management team of people who could run their own shows elsewhere. No, you just need an army of good soldiers who can help implement your great ideas. However, when the genius leaves, the helpers are often lost. Or, worse, they try to mimic their predecessor with bold, visionary moves (trying to act like a genius, without being a genius) that prove unsuccessful.

Eckerd Corporation suffered the liability of a leader who had an uncanny genius for figuring out "what" to do but little ability to assemble the right "who" on the executive team. Jack Eckerd, blessed with monumental personal energy (he campaigned for governor of Florida while running his company) and a genetic gift for market insight and shrewd deal making, acquired his way from two little stores in Wilmington, Delaware, to a drugstore empire of over a thousand stores spread across the southeastern United States. By the late 1970s, Eckerd's revenues equaled Walgreens', and it looked like Eckerd might triumph as the great company in the industry. But then Jack Eckerd left to pursue his passion for politics, running for senator and joining the Ford administration in Washington. Without his guiding genius, Eckerd's company began a long decline, eventually being acquired by J. C. Penney.[18]

The contrast between Jack Eckerd and Cork Walgreen is striking. Whereas Jack Eckerd had a genius for picking the right stores to buy, Cork Walgreen had a genius for picking the right people to hire.[19] Whereas Jack Eckerd had a gift for seeing which stores should go in what locations, Cork Walgreen had a gift for seeing which people should go in what seats. Whereas Jack Eckerd failed utterly at the single most important decision facing any executive—the selection of a successor—Cork Walgreen developed multiple outstanding candidates and selected a superstar successor, who may prove to be even better than Cork himself.[20] Whereas Jack Eckerd had no executive team, but instead a bunch of capable helpers assembled to assist the great genius, Cork Walgreen built the best executive team in the industry. Whereas the primary guidance mechanism for Eckerd Corporation's strategy lay inside Jack Eckerd's head, the primary guidance mechanism for Walgreens' corporate strategy lay in the group dialogue and shared insights of the talented executive team.

LEVEL 5 + MANAGEMENT TEAM (Good-to-Great Companies)	A "GENIUS WITH A THOUSAND HELPERS" (Comparison Companies)
LEVEL 5 LEADER ↓	**LEVEL 4 LEADER** ↓
FIRST WHO Get the right people on the bus. Build a superior executive team. ↓	**FIRST WHAT** Set a vision for where to drive the bus. Develop a road map for driving the bus. ↓
THEN WHAT Once you have the right people in place, figure out the best path to greatness.	**THEN WHO** Enlist a crew of highly capable "helpers" to make the vision happen.

The "genius with a thousand helpers" model is particularly prevalent in the unsustained comparison companies. The most classic case comes from a man known as the Sphinx, Henry Singleton of Teledyne. Singleton grew up on a Texas ranch, with the childhood dream of becoming a great businessman in the model of the rugged individualist. Armed with a Ph.D. from MIT, he founded Teledyne.[21] The name Teledyne derives from Greek and means "force applied at a distance"—an apt name, as the central force holding the far-flung empire together was Henry Singleton himself.

Through acquisitions, Singleton built the company from a small enterprise to number 293 on the Fortune 500 list in six years.[22] Within ten years, he'd completed more than 100 acquisitions, eventually creating a far-flung enterprise with 130 profit centers in everything from exotic metals to insurance.[23] Amazingly, the whole system worked, with Singleton himself acting as the glue that connected all the moving parts together. At one point, he said, "I define my job as having the freedom to do what seems to me to be in the best interest of the company at any time."[24] A 1978 *Forbes* feature story maintained, "Singleton will win no awards for humility, but who can avoid standing in awe of his impressive record?" Singleton continued to run the company well into his seventies, with no serious thought given to succession. After all, why worry about succession when the very point of the whole thing is to serve as a platform to leverage the talents of your remarkable genius? "If there is a single weakness in this otherwise brilliant picture," the article continued, "it is this: Teledyne is not so much a system as it is the reflection of one man's singular discipline."[25]

TELEDYNE CORPORATION
A Classic "Genius with a Thousand Helpers"
Ratio of Cumulative Stock Returns to General Market,
January 1, 1967 – January 1, 1996

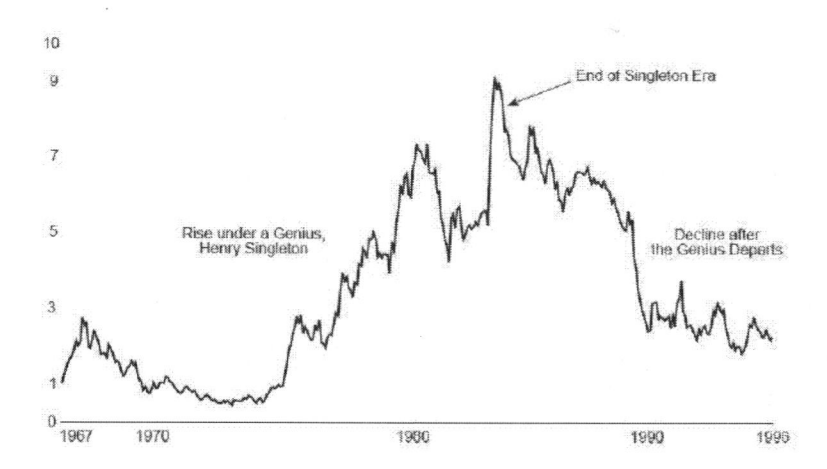

What a weakness it turned out to be. Once Singleton stepped away from day-to-day management in the mid-1980s, the far-flung empire began to crumble. From the end of 1986 until its merger with Allegheny in 1995, Teledyne's cumulative stock returns imploded, falling 66 percent behind the general stock market. Singleton achieved his childhood dream of becoming a great businessman, but he failed utterly at the task of building a great company.

IT'S WHO YOU PAY, NOT HOW YOU PAY THEM

We expected to find that changes in incentive systems, especially executive incentives, would be highly correlated with making the leap from good to great. With all the attention paid to executive compensation—the shift to stock options and the huge packages that have become common-place—surely, we thought, the amount and structure of compensation must play a key role in going from good to great. How else do you get people to do the right things that create great results?

We were dead wrong in our expectations.

> We found no systematic pattern linking executive compensation to the process of going from good to great. The evidence simply does not support the idea that the specific structure of executive compensation acts as a key lever in taking a company from good to great.

We spent weeks inputting compensation data from proxy statements and performed 112 separate analyses looking for patterns and correlations. We examined everything we could quantify for the top five officers—cash versus stock, long-term versus short-term incentives, salary versus bonus, and so forth. Some companies used stock extensively; others didn't. Some had high salaries; others didn't. Some made significant use of bonus incentives; others didn't. Most importantly, when we analyzed executive compensation patterns *relative to comparison companies, we found no systematic differences* on the use of stock (or not), high salaries (or not), bonus incentives (or not), or long-term compensation (or not). The only significant difference we found was that the good-to-great executives received slightly *less* total cash compensation ten years after the transition than their counterparts at the still-mediocre comparison companies![26]

Not that executive compensation is irrelevant. You have to be basically rational and reasonable (I doubt that Colman Mockler, David Maxwell, or Darwin Smith would have worked for free), and the good-to-great companies did spend time thinking about the issue. But once you've structured something that makes basic sense, executive compensation falls away as a distinguishing variable in moving an organization from good to great.

Why might that be? It is simply a manifestation of the "first who" principle: *It's not how you compensate your executives, it's which executives you have to compensate in the first place.* If you have the right executives on the bus, they will do everything within their power to build a great company, not because of what they will "get" for it, but because they simply cannot imagine settling for anything less. Their moral code requires building excellence for its own sake, and you're no more likely to change that with a compensation package than you're likely to affect whether they breathe. The good-to-great companies understood a simple truth: The right people will do the right things and deliver the best results they're capable of, regardless of the incentive system.

> Yes, compensation and incentives are important, but for very different reasons in good-to-great companies. The purpose of a compensation system should not be to get the right *behaviors* from the wrong people, but to get the right *people* on the bus in the first place, and to keep them there.

We were not able to look as rigorously at nonexecutive compensation; such data is not available in as systematic a format as proxy statements for top officers. Nonetheless, evidence from source documents and articles suggests that the same idea applies at all levels of an organization.[27]

A particularly vivid example is Nucor. Nucor built its entire system on the idea that you can teach farmers how to make steel, but you can't teach a farmer work ethic to people who don't have it in the first place. So, instead of setting up mills in traditional steel towns like Pittsburgh and Gary, it located its plants in places like Crawfordsville, Indiana; Norfolk, Nebraska; and Plymouth, Utah— places full of real farmers who go to bed early, rise at dawn, and get right to work without fanfare. "Gotta milk the cows" and "Gonna plow the north forty before noon" translated easily into "Gotta roll some sheet steel" and "Gonna cast forty tons before lunch." Nucor ejected people who did not share this work ethic, generating as high as 50 percent turnover in the first year of a plant, followed by very low turnover as the right people settled in for the long haul.[28]

To attract and keep the best workers, Nucor paid its steelworkers more than any other steel company in the world. But it built its pay system around a high-pressure team-bonus mechanism, with over 50 percent of a worker's compensation tied directly to the productivity of his work team of twenty to forty people.[29] Nucor team members would usually show up for work thirty minutes early to arrange their tools and prepare to blast off the starting line the instant the shift gun fired.[30] "We have the hardest working steel workers in the world," said one Nucor executive. "We hire five, work them like ten, and pay them like eight."[31]

The Nucor system did not aim to turn lazy people into hard workers, but to create an environment where hardworking people would thrive and lazy workers would either jump or get thrown right off the bus. In one extreme case, workers chased a lazy teammate right out of the plant with an angle iron.[32]

> Nucor rejected the old adage that people are your most important asset. In a good-to-great transformation, people are not your most important asset. The *right* people are.

Nucor illustrates a key point. In determining "the right people," the good-to-great companies placed greater weight on character attributes than on specific educational background, practical skills, specialized knowledge, or work experience. Not that specific knowledge or skills are unimportant, but they viewed these traits as more teachable (or at least learnable), whereas they believed dimensions like character, work ethic, basic intelligence, dedication to fulfilling commitments, and values are more ingrained. As Dave Nassef of Pitney Bowes put it:

> I used to be in the Marines, and the Marines get a lot of credit for building people's values. But that's not the way it really works. The Marine Corps recruits people who share the corps' values, then provides them with the training required to accomplish the organization's mission. We look at it the same way at Pitney Bowes. We have more people who want to do the right thing than most companies. We don't just look at experience. We want to know: Who are they? Why are they? We find out who they are by asking them why they made decisions in their life. The answers to these questions give us insight into their core values.[33]

One good-to-great executive said that his best hiring decisions often came from people with no industry or business experience. In one case, he hired a manager who'd been captured twice during the Second World War and escaped both times. "I thought that anyone who could do that shouldn't have trouble with business."[34]

RIGOROUS, NOT RUTHLESS

The good-to-great companies probably sound like tough places to work— and they are. If you don't have what it takes, you probably won't last long. But they're not ruthless cultures, they're rigorous cultures. And the distinction is crucial.

To be ruthless means hacking and cutting, especially in difficult times, or wantonly firing people without any thoughtful consideration. To be rigorous means consistently applying exacting standards at all times and at all levels, especially in upper management. To be rigorous, not ruthless, means that the best people need not worry about their positions and can concentrate fully on their work.

In 1986, Wells Fargo acquired Crocker Bank and planned to shed gobs of excess cost in the consolidation. There's nothing unusual about that— every bank merger in the era of deregulation aimed to cut excess cost out of a bloated and protected industry. However, what *was* unusual about the Wells-Crocker consolidation is the way Wells integrated management or, to be more accurate, the way it didn't even try to integrate most Crocker management into the Wells culture.

The Wells Fargo team concluded right up front that the vast majority of Crocker managers would be the wrong people on the bus. Crocker people had long been steeped in the traditions and perks of old-style banker culture, complete with a marbled executive dining room with its own chef and $500,000 worth of china.[35] Quite a contrast to the spartan culture at Wells Fargo, where management ate food prepared by a college dormitory food service.[36] Wells Fargo made it clear to the Crocker managers: "Look, this is not a merger of equals; it's an acquisition; we bought your branches and your customers; we didn't acquire *you*." Wells Fargo terminated most of the Crocker management team—1,600 Crocker managers gone on day one—including nearly all the top executives.[37]

A critic might say, "That's just the Wells people protecting their *own*." But consider the following fact: Wells Fargo also sent some of its *own* managers packing in cases where the Crocker managers were judged as better qualified. When it came to management, the Wells Fargo standards were ferocious and consistent. Like a professional sports team, only the best made the annual cut, regardless of position or tenure. Summed up one Wells Fargo executive: "The only way to deliver to the people who are achieving is to not burden them with the people who are not achieving."[38]

On the surface, this looks ruthless. But the evidence suggests that the average Crocker manager was just not the same caliber as the average Wells manager and would have failed in the Wells Fargo performance culture. If they weren't going to make it on the bus in the long term, why let them suffer in the short term? One senior Wells Fargo executive told us: "We all agreed this was an acquisition, not a merger, and there's no sense beating around the bush, not being straightforward with people. We decided it would be best to simply do it on day one. We planned our efforts so that we could say, right up front, 'Sorry, we don't see a role for you,' or 'Yes, we do see a role; you have a job, so stop worrying about it.' We were not going to subject our culture to a death by a thousand cuts.' "[39]

To let people languish in uncertainty for months or years, stealing precious time in their lives that they could use to move on to something else, when in the end they aren't going to make it anyway—*that* would be ruthless. To deal with it right up front and let people get on with their lives— that is *rigorous*.

Not that the Crocker acquisition is easy to swallow. It's never pleasant to see thousands of people lose their jobs, but the era of bank deregulation saw hundreds of thousands of lost jobs. Given that, it's interesting to note two points. First, Wells Fargo did fewer big layoffs than its comparison company, Bank of America.[40] Second, upper management, including some senior Wells Fargo upper management, suffered more on a percentage basis than lower-level workers in the consolidation.[41] Rigor in a good-to-great company applies first at the top, focused on those who hold the largest burden of responsibility.

To be rigorous in people decisions means first becoming rigorous about *top management* people decisions. Indeed, I fear that people might use "first who rigor" as an excuse for mindlessly chopping out people to improve performance. "It's hard to do, but we've got to be rigorous," I can hear them say. And I cringe. For not only will a lot of hardworking, good people get hurt in the process, but the evidence suggests that such tactics are contrary to producing sustained great results. The good-to-great companies rarely used head-count lopping as a tactic and almost never used it as a primary strategy. Even in the Wells Fargo case, the company used layoffs *half as* much as Bank of America during the transition era.

> Six of the eleven good-to-great companies recorded zero layoffs from ten years before the breakthrough date all the way through 1998, and four others reported only one or two layoffs.

In contrast, we found layoffs used five times more frequently in the comparison companies than in the good-to-great companies. Some of the comparison companies had an almost chronic addiction to layoffs and restructurings.[42]

It would be a mistake—a tragic mistake, indeed—to think that the way you ignite a transition from good to great is by wantonly swinging the ax on vast numbers of hardworking people. Endless restructuring and mindless hacking were never part of the good-to-great model.

How to Be Rigorous

We've extracted three practical disciplines from the research for being rigorous rather than ruthless.

Practical Discipline #1: When in doubt, don't hire—keep looking.
One of the immutable laws of management physics is "Packard's Law." (So called because we first learned it in a previous research project from David Packard, cofounder of the Hewlett-Packard Company.) It goes like this: No company can grow revenues consistently faster than its ability to get enough of the right people to implement that growth and still become a great company. If your growth rate in revenues consistently outpaces your growth rate in people, you simply will not—indeed cannot—build a great company.

> Those who build great companies understand that the ultimate throttle on growth for any great company is not markets, or technology, or competition, or products. It is one thing above all others: the ability to get and keep enough of the right people.

The management team at Circuit City instinctively understood Packard's Law. Driving around Santa Barbara the day after Christmas a few years ago, I noticed something different about the Circuit City store. Other stores had signs and banners reaching out to customers: "Always the Best Prices" or "Great After-Holiday Deals" or "Best After-Christmas Selection," and so forth. But not Circuit City. It had a banner that read: "Always Looking for Great People."

The sign reminded me of our interview with Walter Bruckart, vice president during the good-to-great years. When asked to name the top five factors that led to the transition from mediocrity to excellence, Bruckart said, "One would be people. Two would be people. Three would be people. Four would be people. And five would be people. A huge part of our transition can be attributed to our discipline in picking the right people." Bruckart then recalled a conversation with CEO Alan Wurtzel during a growth spurt at Circuit City: " 'Alan, I'm really wearing down trying to find the exact right person to fill this position or that position. At what point do I compromise?' Without hesitation, Alan said, 'You don't compromise. We find another way to get through until we find the right people.' "[43]

One of the key contrasts between Alan Wurtzel at Circuit City and Sidney Cooper at Silo is that Wurtzel spent the bulk of his time in the early years focused on getting the right people on the bus, whereas Cooper spent 80 percent of his time focusing on the right stores to buy.[44] Wurtzel's first goal was to build the best, most professional management team in the industry; Cooper's first goal was simply to grow as fast as possible. Circuit City put tremendous emphasis on getting the right people all up and down the line, from delivery drivers to vice presidents; Silo developed a reputation for not being able to do the basics, like making home deliveries without damaging the products.[45] According to Circuit City's Dan Rexinger, "We made the best home delivery drivers in the industry. We told them, 'You are the last contact the customer has with Circuit City. We are going to supply you with uniforms. We will require that you shave, that you don't have B.O. You're going to be professional people.' The change in the way we handled customers when making a delivery was absolutely incredible. We would get thank-you notes back on how courteous the drivers were."[46] Five years into Wurtzel's tenure, Circuit City and Silo had essentially the same business strategy (the same answers to the "what" questions), yet Circuit City took off like a rocket, beating the general stock market 18.5 to 1 in the fifteen years after its transition, while Silo bumped along until it was finally acquired by a foreign company.[47] Same strategy, different people, different results.

Practical Discipline #2: When you know you need to make a people change, act. The moment you feel the need to tightly manage someone, you've made a hiring mistake. The best people don't need to be managed. Guided, taught, led—yes. But not tightly managed. We've all experienced or observed the following scenario. We have a wrong person on the bus and we know it. Yet we wait, we delay, we try alternatives, we give a third and fourth chance, we hope that the situation will improve, we invest time in trying to properly manage the person, we build little systems to compensate for his shortcomings, and so forth. But the situation doesn't improve. When we go home, we find our energy diverted by thinking (or talking to our spouses) about that person. Worse, all the time and energy we spend on that one person siphons energy away from developing and working with all the right people. We continue to stumble along until the person leaves on his own (to our great sense of relief) or we finally act (also to our great sense of relief). Meanwhile, our best people wonder, "What took you so long?"

Letting the wrong people hang around is unfair to all the right people, as they inevitably find themselves compensating for the inadequacies of the wrong people. Worse, it can drive away the best people. Strong performers are intrinsically motivated by performance, and when they see their efforts impeded by carrying extra weight, they eventually become frustrated.

Waiting too long before acting is equally unfair to the people who need to get off the bus. For every minute you allow a person to continue holding a seat when you know that person will not make it in the end, you're stealing a portion of his life, time that he could spend finding a better place where he could flourish. Indeed, if we're honest with ourselves, the reason we wait too long often has less to do with concern for that person and more to do with our own convenience. He's doing an okay job and it would be a huge hassle to replace him, so we avoid the issue. Or we find the whole process of dealing with the issue to be stressful and distasteful. So, to save ourselves stress and discomfort, we wait. And wait. And wait. Meanwhile, all the best people are still wondering, "When are they going to do something about this? How long is this going to go on?"

Using data from *Moody's Company Information Reports*, we were able to examine the pattern of turnover in the top management levels. We found no difference in the *amount* of "churn" (turnover within a period of time) between the good-to-great and the comparison companies. But we did find differences in the *pattern* of churn.[48]

> The good-to-great companies showed the following bipolar pattern at the top management level: People either stayed on the bus for a long time or got off the bus in a hurry. In other words, the good-to-great companies did not churn more, they churned *better*.

The good-to-great leaders did not pursue an expedient "try a lot of people and keep who works" model of management. Instead, they adopted the following approach: "Let's take the time to make rigorous A+ selections right up front. If we get it right, we'll do everything we can to try to keep them on board for a long time. If we make a mistake, then we'll confront that fact so that we can get on with our work and they can get on with their lives."

The good-to-great leaders, however, would not rush to judgment. Often, they invested substantial effort in determining whether they had someone in the wrong seat before concluding that they had the wrong person on the bus entirely. When Colman Mockler became CEO of Gillette, he didn't go on a rampage, wantonly throwing people out the windows of a moving bus. Instead, he spent fully 55 percent of his time during his first two years in office jiggering around with the management team, changing or moving thirty-eight of the top fifty people. Said Mockler, "Every minute devoted to putting the proper person in the proper slot is worth weeks of time later."[49] Similarly, Alan Wurtzel of Circuit

City sent us a letter after reading an early draft of this chapter, wherein he commented:

> Your point about "getting the right people on the bus" as compared to other companies is dead on. There is one corollary that is also important. I spent a lot of time thinking and talking about who sits where on the bus. I called it "putting square pegs in square holes and round pegs in round holes."... Instead of firing honest and able people who are not performing well, it is important to try to move them once or even two or three times to other positions where they might blossom.

It might take time to know for certain if someone is simply in the wrong seat or whether he needs to get off the bus altogether. Nonetheless, when the good-to-great leaders knew they had to make a people change, they would *act*.

But how do you know when you *know*? Two key questions can help. First, if it were a hiring decision (rather than a "should this person get off the bus?" decision), would you hire the person again? Second, if the person came to tell you that he or she is leaving to pursue an exciting new opportunity, would you feel terribly disappointed or secretly relieved?

Practical Discipline #3: Put your best people on your biggest opportunities, not your biggest problems.
In the early 1960s, R. J. Reynolds and Philip Morris derived the vast majority of their revenues from the domestic arena. R. J. Reynolds' approach to international business was, "If somebody out there in the world wants a Camel, let them call us."[50] Joe Cullman at Philip Morris had a different view. He identified international markets as the single best opportunity for long-term growth, despite the fact that the company derived less than 1 percent of its revenues from overseas.

Cullman puzzled over the best "strategy" for developing international operations and eventually came up with a brilliant answer: It was not a "what" answer, but a "who." He pulled his number one executive, George Weissman, off the primary domestic business, and put him in charge of international. At the time, international amounted to almost nothing—a tiny export department, a struggling investment in Venezuela, another in Australia, and a tiny operation in Canada. "When Joe put George in charge of international, a lot of people wondered what George had done wrong," quipped one of Weissman's colleagues.[51] "I didn't know whether I was being thrown sideways, downstairs or out the window," said Weissman. "Here I was running 99% of the company and the next day I'd be running 1% or less."[52]

Yet, as *Forbes* magazine observed twenty years later, Cullman's decision to move Weissman to the smallest part of the business was a stroke of genius. Urbane and sophisticated, Weissman was the perfect person to develop markets like Europe, and he built international into the largest and fastest-growing part of the company. In fact, under Weissman's stewardship, Marlboro became the bestselling cigarette *in the world* three years *before* it became number one in the United States.[53]

The RJR versus Philip Morris case illustrates a common pattern. The good-to-great companies made a habit of putting their best people on their best opportunities, not their biggest problems. The comparison companies had a penchant for doing just the opposite, failing to grasp the fact that managing your problems can only make you good, whereas building your opportunities is the only way to become great.

> There is an important corollary to this discipline: *When you decide to sell off your problems, don't sell off your best people.* This is one of those little secrets of change. If you create a place where the best people always have a seat on the bus, they're more likely to support changes in direction.

For instance, when Kimberly-Clark sold the mills, Darwin Smith made it clear: The company might be getting rid of the paper business, *but it would keep its best people.* "*Many of our people* had come up through the paper business. Then, all of a sudden, the crown jewels are being sold off and they're asking, 'What is my future?' " explained Dick Auchter. "And Darwin would say, 'We need all the talented managers we can get. We keep them.' "[54] Despite the fact that they had little or no consumer experience, Smith moved all the best paper people to the consumer business.

We interviewed Dick Appert, a senior executive who spent the majority of his career in the papermaking division at Kimberly-Clark, the same division sold off to create funds for the company's big move into consumer products. He talked with pride and excitement about the transformation of Kimberly-Clark, how it had the guts to sell the paper mills, how it had the foresight to exit the paper business and throw the proceeds into the consumer business, and how it had taken on Procter & Gamble. "I never had any argument with our decision to dissolve the paper division of the company," he said. "We did get rid of the paper mills at that time, and I was in absolute agreement with that."[55] Stop and think about that for a moment. The right people want to be part of building something great, and Dick Appert saw that Kimberly-Clark could become great by selling the part of the company where he had spent most of his working life.

The Philip Morris and Kimberly-Clark cases illustrate a final point about "the right people." We noticed a Level 5 atmosphere at the top executive level of every good-to-great company, especially during the key transition years. Not that every executive on the team became a fully evolved Level 5 leader to the same degree as Darwin Smith or Colman Mockler, but each core member of the team transformed personal ambition into ambition for the company. This suggests that the team members had Level 5 potential—or at least they were capable of operating in a manner consistent with the Level 5 leadership style.

You might be wondering, "What's the difference between a Level 5 executive team member and just being a good soldier?" A Level 5 executive team member does not blindly acquiesce to authority and is a strong leader in her own right, so driven and talented that she builds her arena into one of the very best in the world. Yet each team member must also have the ability to meld that strength into doing whatever it takes to make the company great.

> Indeed, one of the crucial elements in taking a company from good to great is somewhat paradoxical. You need executives, on the one hand, who argue and debate—sometimes violently—in pursuit of the best answers, yet, on the other hand, who unify fully behind a decision, regardless of parochial interests.

An article on Philip Morris said of the Cullman era, "These guys never agreed on anything and they would argue about everything, and they would kill each other and involve everyone, high and low, talented people. But when they had to make a decision, the decision would emerge. This made Philip Morris."[56] No matter how much they argued, said a Philip Morris executive, "they were always in search of the best answer. In the end, everybody stood behind the decision. All of the debates were for the common good of the company, not your own interests."[57]

FIRST WHO, GREAT COMPANIES, AND A GREAT LIFE

Whenever I teach the good-to-great findings, someone almost always raises the issue of the personal cost in making a transition from good to great. In other words, is it possible to build a great company and also build a great life?

Yes.

The secret to doing so lies right in this chapter.

I spent a few short days with a senior Gillette executive and his wife at an executive conference in Hong Kong. During the course of our conversations, I asked them if they thought Colman Mockler, the CEO most responsible for Gillette's transition from good to great, had a great life. Colman's life revolved around three great loves, they told me: his family, Harvard, and Gillette. Even during the darkest and most intense times of the takeover crises of the 1980s and despite the increasingly global nature of Gillette's business, Mockler maintained remarkable balance in his life. He did not significantly reduce the amount of time he spent with his family, rarely working evenings or weekends. He maintained his disciplined worship practices. He continued his active work on the governing board of Harvard College.[58]

When I asked how Mockler accomplished all of this, the executive said, "Oh, it really wasn't that hard for him. He was so good at assembling the right people around him, and putting the right people in the right slots, that he just didn't need to be there all hours of the day and night. That was Colman's whole secret to success and balance." The executive went on to explain that he was just as likely to meet Mockler in the hardware store as at the office. "He really enjoyed puttering around the house, fixing things up. He always seemed to find time to relax that way." Then the executive's wife added, "When Colman died and we all went to the funeral, I looked around and realized how much love was in the room. This was a man who spent nearly all his waking hours with people who loved him, who loved what they were doing, and who loved one another—at work, at home, in his charitable work, wherever."

And the statement rang a bell for me, as there was something about the good-to-great executive teams that I couldn't quite describe, but that clearly set them apart. In wrapping up our interview with George Weissman of Philip Morris, I commented, "When you talk about your time at the company, it's as if you are describing a love affair." He chuckled and said, "Yes. Other than my marriage, it was *the* passionate love affair of my life. I don't think many people would understand what I'm talking about, but I suspect my colleagues would." Weissman and many of his executive colleagues kept offices at Philip Morris, coming in on a regular basis, long after retirement. A corridor at the Philip Morris world headquarters is called "the hall of the wizards of was."[59] It's the corridor where Weissman, Cullman, Maxwell, and others continue to come into the office, in large part because they simply enjoy spending time together. Similarly, Dick Appert of Kimberly-Clark said in his interview, "I never had anyone in Kimberly-Clark in all my forty-one years say anything unkind to me. I thank God the day I was hired because I've been associated with wonderful people. Good, good people who respected and admired one another."[60]

Members of the good-to-great teams tended to become and remain friends for life. In many cases, they are still in close contact with each other years or decades after working together. It was striking to hear them talk about the transition era, for no matter how dark the days or how big the tasks, these people had fun! They enjoyed each other's company and actually looked forward to meetings. A number of the executives characterized their years on the good-to-great teams as the high point of their lives. Their experiences went beyond just mutual respect (which they certainly had), to lasting comradeship.

Adherence to the idea of "first who" might be the closest link between a great company and a great life. For no matter what we achieve, if we don't spend the vast majority of our time with people we love and respect, we cannot possibly have a great life. But if we spend the vast majority of our time with people we love and respect—people we really enjoy being on the bus with and who will never disappoint us—then we will almost certainly have a great life, no matter where the bus goes. The people we interviewed from the good-to-great companies clearly loved what they did, largely because they loved who they did it with.

Chapter Summary
First Who ... Then What

KEY POINTS

• The good-to-great leaders began the transformation by first getting the right people on the bus (and the wrong people off the bus) and then figured out where to drive it.

• The key point of this chapter is *not* just the idea of getting the right people on the team. The key point is that "who" questions come before "what" decisions—before vision, before strategy, before organization structure, before tactics. *First* who, *then* what—as a rigorous discipline, consistently applied.

• The comparison companies frequently followed the "genius with a thousand helpers" model—a genius leader who sets a vision and then enlists a crew of highly capable "helpers" to make the vision happen. This model fails when the genius departs.

• The good-to-great leaders were rigorous, not ruthless, in people decisions. They did not rely on layoffs and restructuring as a primary strategy for improving performance. The comparison companies used layoffs to a much greater extent.

• We uncovered three practical disciplines for being rigorous in people decisions:

1. When in doubt, don't hire—keep looking. (*Corollary*: A company should limit its growth based on its ability to attract enough of the right people.)

2. When you know you need to make a people change, act. (*Corollary*: First be sure you don't simply have someone in the wrong seat.)

3. Put your best people on your biggest opportunities, not your biggest problems. (*Corollary*: If you sell off your problems, don't sell off your

best people.)

- Good-to-great management teams consist of people who debate vigorously in search of the best answers, yet who unify behind decisions, regardless of parochial interests.

UNEXPECTED FINDINGS

- We found no systematic pattern linking executive compensation to the shift from good to great. The purpose of compensation is not to "motivate" the right behaviors from the wrong people, but to get and keep the right people in the first place.
- The old adage "People are your most important asset" is wrong. People are not your most important asset. The *right* people are.
- Whether someone is the "right person" has more to do with character traits and innate capabilities than with specific knowledge, background, or skills.

CHAPTER 4
Confront The Brutal Facts (Yet Never Lose Faith)

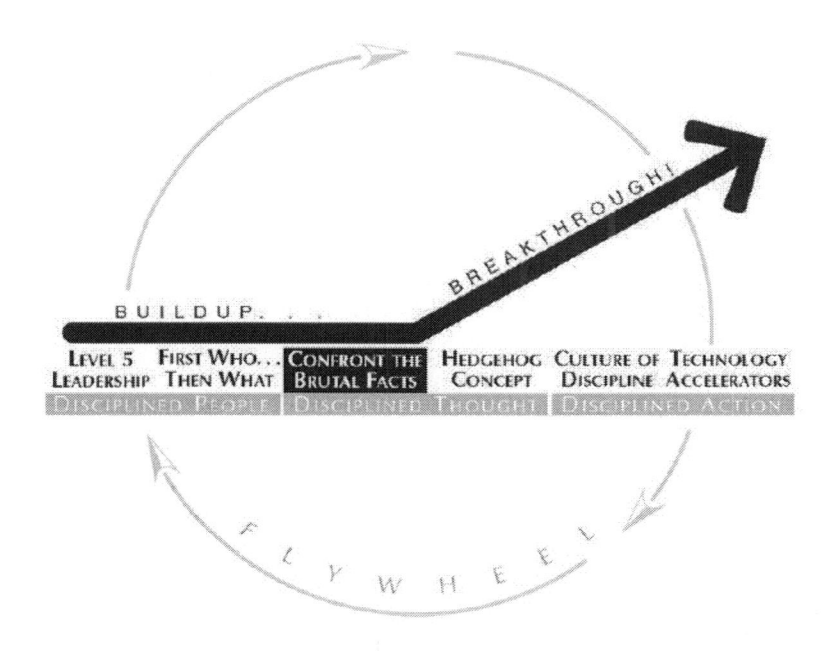

> There is no worse mistake in public leadership than to hold out false hopes soon to be swept away.
>
> —Winston S. Churchill,
> *The Hinge of Fate*[1]

In the early 1950s, the Great Atlantic and Pacific Tea Company, commonly known as A&P, stood as the largest retailing organization in the world and one of the largest corporations in the United States, at one point ranking behind only General Motors in annual sales.[2] Kroger, in contrast, stood as an unspectacular grocery chain, less than half the size of A&P, with performance that barely kept pace with the general market.

Then in the 1960s, A&P began to falter while Kroger began to lay the foundations for a transition into a great company. From 1959 to 1973, both companies lagged behind the market, with Kroger pulling just a bit ahead of

A&P. After that, the two companies completely diverged, and over the next twenty-five years, Kroger generated cumulative returns *ten times the market* and *eighty* times better than A&P.

How did such a dramatic reversal of fortunes happen? And how could a company as great as A&P become so awful?

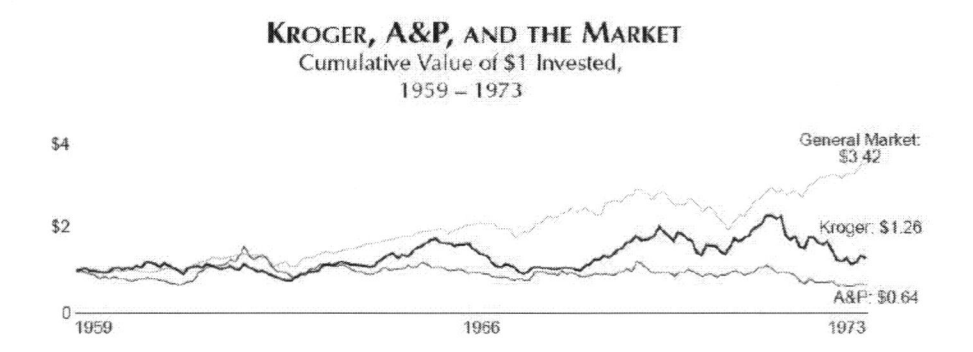

KROGER, A&P, AND THE MARKET
Cumulative Value of $1 Invested,
1959 – 1973

General Market: $3.42
Kroger: $1.26
A&P: $0.64

Notes:

1. Kroger transition point occurred in 1973.
2. Chart shows value of $1 invested on January 1, 1959.
3. Cumulative returns, dividends reinvested, to January 1, 1973.

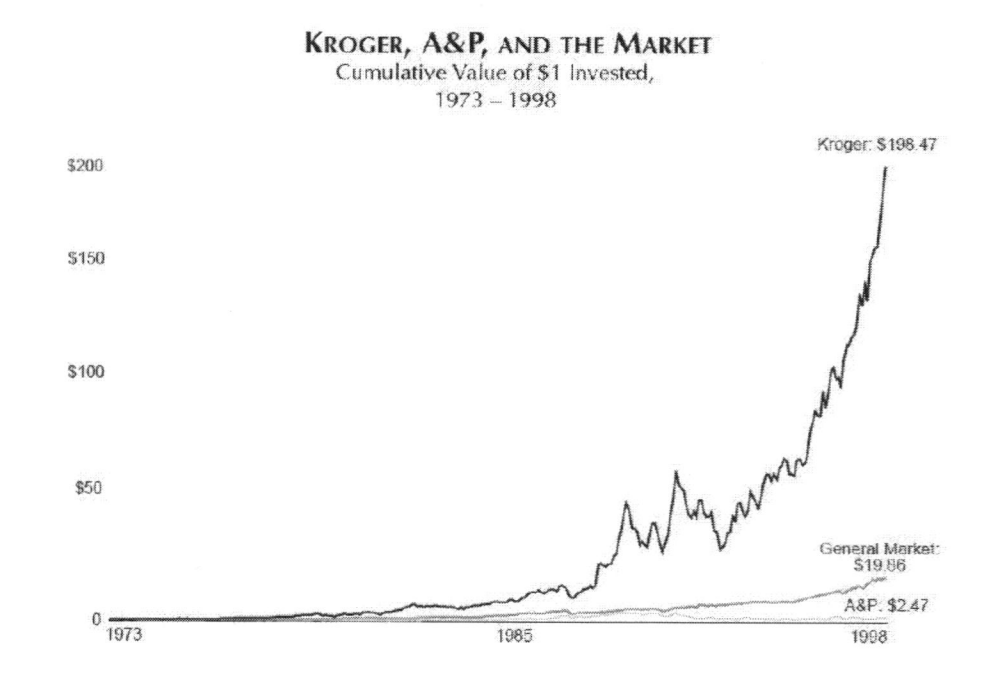

KROGER, A&P, AND THE MARKET
Cumulative Value of $1 Invested,
1973 – 1998

Kroger: $198.47
General Market: $19.86
A&P: $2.47

Notes:

1. Kroger transition point occurred in 1973.

2. Chart shows value of $1 invested on January 1, 1973.
3. Cumulative returns, dividends reinvested, to January 1, 1998.

A&P had a perfect model for the first half of the twentieth century, when two world wars and a depression imposed frugality upon Americans: cheap, plentiful groceries sold in utilitarian stores. But in the affluent second half of the twentieth century, Americans changed. They wanted nicer stores, bigger stores, more choices in stores. They wanted fresh-baked bread, flowers, health foods, cold medicines, fresh produce, forty-five choices of cereal, and ten types of milk. They wanted offbeat items, like five different types of expensive sprouts and various concoctions of protein powder and Chinese healing herbs. Oh, and they wanted to be able to do their banking and get their annual flu shots while shopping. In short, they no longer wanted grocery stores. They wanted Superstores, with a big block "S" on the chest—offering almost everything under one roof, with lots of parking, cheap prices, clean floors, and a gazillion checkout lines.

Now, right off the bat, you might be thinking: "Okay, so the story of A&P is one of an aging company that had a strategy that was right for the times, but the times changed and the world passed it by as younger, better-attuned companies gave customers more of what they wanted. What's so interesting about that?"

Here's what's interesting: *Both* Kroger and A&P were old companies (Kroger at 82 years, A&P at 111 years) heading into the 1970s; *both* companies had nearly all their assets invested in traditional grocery stores; *both* companies had strongholds outside the major growth areas of the United States; and *both* companies had knowledge of how the world around them was changing. Yet one of these two companies confronted the brutal facts of reality head-on and completely changed its entire system in response; the other stuck its head in the sand.

In 1958, *Forbes* magazine described A&P as "the Hermit Kingdom," run as an absolute monarchy by an aging prince.[3] Ralph Burger, the successor to the Hartford brothers who had built the A&P dynasty, sought to preserve two things above all else: cash dividends for the family foundation and the past glory of the Hartford brothers. According to one A&P director, Burger "considered himself the reincarnation of old John Hartford, even to the point of wearing a flower in his lapel every day from Hartford's greenhouse. He tried to carry out, against all opposition, what he thought Mr. John [Hartford] would have liked."[4] Burger instilled a "what would Mr. Hartford do?" approach to decisions, living by the motto "You can't argue with a hundred years of success."[5] Indeed, through Burger, Mr. Hartford continued to be the dominant force on the board for nearly twenty years. Never mind the fact that he was already dead.[6]

As the brutal facts about the mismatch between its past model and the changing world began to pile up, A&P mounted an increasingly spirited defense against those facts. In one series of events, the company opened a new store called The Golden Key, a separate brand wherein it could experiment with new methods and models to learn what customers wanted.[7] It sold no A&P-branded products, it gave the store manager more freedom, it experimented with innovative new departments, and it began to evolve toward the modern superstore. Customers really liked it. Here, right under their noses, they began to discover the answer to the questions of why they were losing market share and what they could do about it.

What did A&P executives do with The Golden Key?

They didn't like the answers that it gave, so they closed it.[8]

A&P then began a pattern of lurching from one strategy to another, always looking for a single-stroke solution to its problems. It held pep rallies, launched programs, grabbed fads, fired CEOs, hired CEOs, and fired them yet again. It launched what one industry observer called a "scorched earth policy," a radical price-cutting strategy to build market share, but never dealt with the basic fact that customers wanted not lower prices, but *different stores*.[9] The price cutting led to cost cutting, which led to even drabber stores and poorer service, which in turn drove customers away, further driving down margins, resulting in even dirtier stores and worse service. "After a while the crud kept mounting," said one former A&P manager. "We not only had dirt, we had dirty dirt."[10]

Meanwhile, over at Kroger, a completely different pattern arose. Kroger also conducted experiments in the 1960s to test the superstore concept.[11] By 1970, the Kroger executive team came to an inescapable conclusion: The old-model grocery store (which accounted for nearly 100 percent of Kroger's business) was going to become extinct. Unlike A&P, however, Kroger confronted this brutal truth and acted on it.

The rise of Kroger is remarkably simple and straightforward, almost maddeningly so. During their interviews, Lyle Everingham and his predecessor Jim Herring (CEOs during the pivotal transition years) were polite and helpful, but a bit exasperated by our questions. To them, it just seemed so clear. When we asked Everingham to allocate one hundred points across the top five factors in the transition, he said: "I find your question a bit perplexing. Basically, we did extensive research, and the data came back loud and clear: The supercombination stores were the way of the future. We also learned that you had to be number one or number two in each market, or you had to exit.[*] Sure, there was some skepticism at first. But once we looked at the facts, there was really no question about what we had to do. So we just did it."[12]

Kroger decided to eliminate, change, or replace every single store and depart every region that did not fit the new realities. The whole system would be turned inside out, store by store, block by block, city by city, state by state. By the early 1990s, Kroger had rebuilt its entire system on the new model and was well on the way to becoming the number one grocery chain in America, a position it would attain in 1999.[13] Meanwhile, A&P *still* had over half its stores in the old 1950s size and had dwindled to a sad remnant of a once-great American institution.[14]

FACTS ARE BETTER THAN DREAMS

One of the dominant themes from our research is that breakthrough results come about by a series of good decisions, diligently executed and accumulated one on top of another. Of course, the good-to-great companies did not have a perfect track record. But on the whole, they made many more good decisions than bad ones, and they made many more good decisions than the comparison companies. Even more important, on the really big choices, such as Kroger's decision to throw all its resources into the task of converting its entire system to the superstore concept, they were remarkably on target.

This, of course, begs a question. Are we merely studying a set of companies that just happened by luck to stumble into the right set of decisions? Or was there something *distinctive* about their process that dramatically increased the likelihood of being right? The answer, it turns out, is that there was something quite distinctive about their process.

The good-to-great companies displayed two distinctive forms of disciplined thought. The first, and the topic of this chapter, is that they infused the entire process with the brutal facts of reality. (The second, which we will discuss in the next chapter, is that they developed a simple, yet deeply insightful, frame of reference for all decisions.) When, as in the Kroger case, you start with an honest and diligent effort to determine the truth of the situation, the right decisions often become self-evident. Not always, of course, but often. And even if all decisions do not become self-evident, one thing is certain: You absolutely cannot make a series of good decisions without first confronting the brutal facts. The good-to-great companies operated in accordance with this principle, and the comparison companies generally did not.

Consider Pitney Bowes versus Addressograph. It would be hard to find two companies in more similar positions at a specific moment in history that then diverged so dramatically. Until 1973, they had similar revenues, profits, numbers of employees, and stock charts. Both companies held near-monopoly market positions with virtually the same customer base— Pitney Bowes in postage meters and Addressograph in address-duplicating machines—and both faced the imminent reality of losing their monopolies.[15] By 2000, however, Pitney Bowes had grown to over 30,000 employees and revenues in excess of $4 billion, compared to the sorry remnants of Addressograph, which had less than $100 million and only 670 employees.[16] For the shareholder, Pitney Bowes outperformed Addressograph 3,581 to 1 (yes, *three thousand five hundred and eighty-one* times better).

In 1976, a charismatic visionary leader named Roy Ash became CEO of Addressograph. A self-described "conglomerateur," Ash had previously built Litton by stacking acquisitions together that had since faltered. According to *Fortune*, he sought to use Addressograph as a platform to reestablish his leadership prowess in the eyes of the world.[17]

Ash set forth a vision to dominate the likes of IBM, Xerox, and Kodak in the emerging field of office automation—a bold plan for a company that had previously only dominated the envelope-address-duplication business.[18] There is nothing wrong with a bold vision, but Ash became so wedded to his quixotic quest that, according to *Business Week*, he refused to confront the mounting evidence that his plan was doomed to fail and might take down the rest of the company with it.[19] He insisted on milking cash from profitable arenas, eroding the core business while throwing money after a gambit that had little chance of success.[20]

Later, after Ash was thrown out of office and the company had filed for bankruptcy (from which it did later emerge), he still refused to confront reality, saying: "We lost some battles, but we were winning the war."[21] But Addressograph was not even close to winning the war, and people throughout the company knew it at the time. Yet the truth went unheard until it was too late.[22] In fact, many of Addressograph's key people bailed out of the company, dispirited by their inability to get top management to deal with the facts.[23]

PITNEY BOWES VERSUS ADDRESSOGRAPH
Annual Revenues, 1963–1998
Constant 1998 Dollars, in Millions

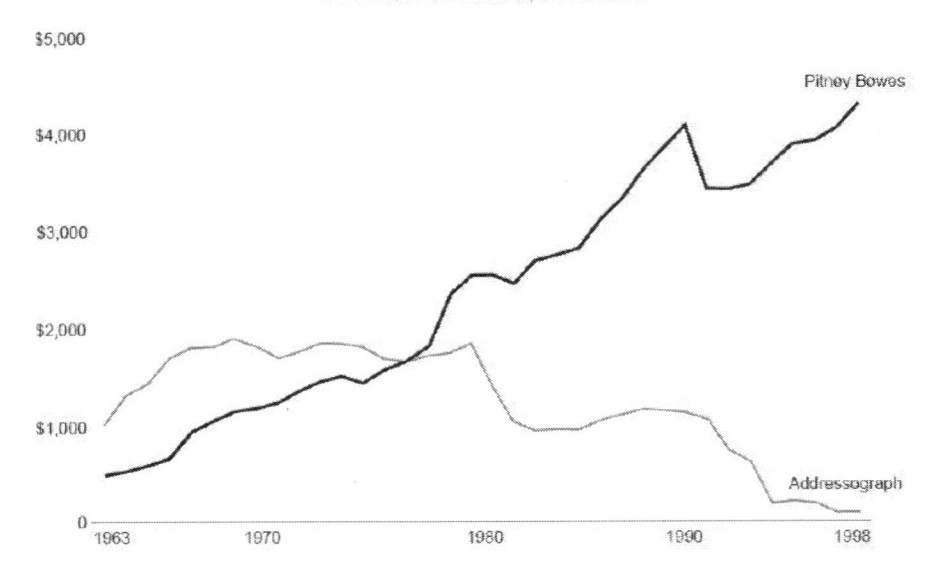

Perhaps we should give Mr. Ash some credit for being a visionary who tried to push his company to greater heights. (And, to be fair, the Addressograph board fired Ash before he had a chance to fully carry out his plans.)[24] But the evidence from a slew of respectable articles written at the time suggests that Ash turned a blind eye to any reality inconsistent with his own vision of the world.

> There is nothing wrong with pursuing a vision for greatness. After all, the good-to-great companies also set out to create greatness. But, unlike the comparison companies, the good-to-great companies continually refined the *path* to greatness with the brutal facts of reality.

"When you turn over rocks and look at all the squiggly things underneath, you can either put the rock down, or you can say, 'My job is to turn over rocks and look at the squiggly things,' even if what you see can scare the hell out of you."[25] That quote, from Pitney Bowes executive Fred Purdue, could have come from any of the Pitney Bowes executives we interviewed. They all seemed a bit, well, to be blunt, neurotic and compulsive about Pitney's position in the world. "This is a culture that is very hostile to complacency," said one executive.[26] "We have an itch that what we just accomplished, no matter how great, is never going to be good enough to sustain us," said another.[27]

Pitney's first management meeting of the new year typically consisted of about fifteen minutes discussing the previous year (almost always superb results) and two hours talking about the "scary squiggly things" that might impede future results.[28] Pitney Bowes sales meetings were quite different from the "aren't we great" rah-rah sales conferences typical at most companies: The entire management team would lay itself open to searing questions and challenges from salespeople who dealt directly with customers.[29] The company created a long-standing tradition of forums where people could stand up and tell senior executives what the company was doing wrong, shoving rocks with squiggly things in their faces, and saying, "Look! You'd better pay attention to this."[30]

The Addressograph case, especially in contrast to Pitney Bowes, illustrates a vital point. Strong, charismatic leaders like Roy Ash can all too easily become the de facto reality driving a company. Throughout the study, we found comparison companies where the top leader led with such force or instilled such fear that people worried more about the leader—what he would say, what he would think, what he would do— than they worried about external reality and what it could do to the company. Recall the climate at Bank of America, described in the previous chapter, wherein managers would not even make a comment until they knew how the CEO felt. We did not find this pattern at companies like Wells Fargo and Pitney Bowes, where people were much more worried about the scary squiggly things than about the feelings of top management.

The moment a leader allows himself to become the primary reality people worry about, rather than reality being the primary reality, you have a recipe for mediocrity, or worse. This is one of the key reasons why less charismatic leaders often produce better long-term results than their more charismatic counterparts.

> Indeed, for those of you with a strong, charismatic personality, it is worthwhile to consider the idea that charisma can be as much a liability as an asset. Your strength of personality can sow the seeds of problems, when people filter the brutal facts from you. You *can* overcome the liabilities of having charisma, but it does require conscious attention.

Winston Churchill understood the liabilities of his strong personality, and he compensated for them beautifully during the Second World War. Churchill, as you know, maintained a bold and unwavering vision that Britain would not just survive, but prevail as a great nation—despite the whole world wondering not if but *when* Britain would sue for peace. During the darkest days, with nearly all of Europe and North Africa under Nazi control, the United States hoping to stay out of the conflict, and Hitler fighting a one-front war (he had not yet turned on Russia), Churchill said: "We are resolved to destroy Hitler and every vestige of the Nazi regime. From this, nothing will turn us. Nothing! We will never parley. We will never negotiate with Hitler or any of his gang. We shall fight him by land. We shall fight him by sea. We shall fight him in the air. Until, with God's help, we have rid the earth of his shadow."[31]

Armed with this bold vision, Churchill never failed, however, to confront the most brutal facts. He feared that his towering, charismatic personality might deter bad news from reaching him in its starkest form. So, early in the war, he created an entirely separate department outside the normal chain of command, called the Statistical Office, with the principal function of feeding him—continuously updated and completely unfiltered—the most brutal facts of reality.[32] He relied heavily on this special unit throughout the war, repeatedly asking for facts, just the facts. As the Nazi panzers swept across Europe, Churchill went to bed and slept soundly: "I... had no need for cheering dreams," he wrote. "*Facts* are better than dreams."[33]

A CLIMATE WHERE THE TRUTH IS HEARD

Now, you might be wondering, "How do you motivate people with brutal facts? Doesn't motivation flow chiefly from a compelling vision?" The answer, surprisingly, is, "*No.*" Not because vision is unimportant, but because expending energy trying to motivate people is largely a waste of time. One of the dominant themes that runs throughout this book is that if you successfully implement its findings, you will not need to spend time and energy "motivating" people. If you have the right people on the bus, they will be self-motivated. The real question then becomes: *How do you manage in such a way as not to de-motivate people?* And one of the single most de-motivating actions you can take is to hold out false hopes, soon to be swept away by events.

> Yes, leadership is about vision. But leadership is equally about creating a climate where the truth is heard and the brutal facts confronted. There's a huge difference between the opportunity to "have your say" and the opportunity to be *heard.* The good-to-great leaders understood this distinction, creating a culture wherein people had a tremendous opportunity

to be heard and, ultimately, for the truth to be heard.

How do you create a climate where the truth is heard? We offer four basic practices:

1. Lead with questions, not answers.
In 1973, one year after he assumed CEO responsibility from his father, Alan Wurtzel's company stood at the brink of bankruptcy, dangerously close to violation of its loan agreements. At the time, the company (then named Wards, not to be confused with Montgomery Ward) was a hodgepodge of appliance and hi-fi stores with no unifying concept. Over the next ten years, Wurtzel and his team not only turned the company around, but also created the Circuit City concept and laid the foundations for a stunning record of results, beating the market twenty-two times from its transition date in 1982 to January 1, 2000.

When Alan Wurtzel started the long traverse from near bankruptcy to these stellar results, he began with a remarkable answer to the question of where to take the company: I *don't know*. Unlike leaders such as Roy Ash of Addressograph, Wurtzel resisted the urge to walk in with "the answer." Instead, once he put the right people on the bus, he began not with answers, but with *questions*. "Alan was a real spark," said a board member. "He had an ability to ask questions that were just marvelous. We had some wonderful debates in the boardroom. It was never just a dog and pony show, where you would just listen and then go to lunch."[34] Indeed, Wurtzel stands as one of the few CEOs in a large corporation who put more questions to his board members than they put to him.

He used the same approach with his executive team, constantly pushing and probing and prodding with questions. Each step along the way, Wurtzel would keep asking questions until he had a clear picture of reality and its implications. "They used to call me the prosecutor, because I would home in on a question," said Wurtzel. "You know, like a bulldog, I wouldn't let go until I understood. Why, why, why?"

Like Wurtzel, leaders in each of the good-to-great transitions operated with a somewhat Socratic style. Furthermore, they used questions for one and only one reason: to gain understanding. They didn't use questions as a form of manipulation ("Don't you agree with me on that? ... ") or as a way to blame or put down others ("Why did you mess this up? ... "). When we asked the executives about their management team meetings during the transition era, they said that they spent much of the time "just trying to understand."

The good-to-great leaders made particularly good use of informal meetings where they'd meet with groups of managers and employees with no script, agenda, or set of action items to discuss. Instead, they would start with questions like: "So, what's on your mind?" "Can you tell me about that?" "Can you help me understand?" "What should we be worried about?" These non-agenda meetings became a forum where current realities tended to bubble to the surface.

> Leading from good to great does not mean coming up with the answers and then motivating everyone to follow your messianic vision. It means having the humility to grasp the fact that you do not yet understand enough to have the answers and then to ask the questions that will lead to the best possible insights.

2. Engage in dialogue and debate, not coercion.
In 1965, you could hardly find a company more awful than Nucor. It had only one division that made money. Everything else drained cash. It had no culture to be proud of. It had no consistent direction. It was on the verge of bankruptcy. At the time, Nucor was officially known as the Nuclear Corporation of America, reflecting its orientation to nuclear energy products, including the Scintillation Probe (yes, they really named it that), used for radiation measurement. It had acquired a series of unrelated businesses in such arenas as semiconductor supplies, rare earth materials, electrostatic office copiers, and roof joists. At the start of its transformation in 1965, Nucor did not manufacture one ounce of steel. Nor did it make a penny of profit. Thirty years later, Nucor stood as the fourth-largest steelmaker in the world[35] and by 1999 made greater annual profits than any other American steel company.[36]

How did Nucor transition from the utterly awful Nuclear Corporation of America into perhaps the best steel company in America? First, Nucor benefited from the emergence of a Level 5 leader, Ken Iverson, promoted to CEO from general manager of the joist division. Second, Iverson got the right people on the bus, building a remarkable team of people like Sam Siegel (described by one of his colleagues as "the best money manager in the world, a magician") and David Aycock, an operations genius.[37]

And then what?

Like Alan Wurtzel, Iverson dreamed of building a great company, but refused to begin with "the answer" for how to get there. Instead, he played the role of Socratic moderator in a series of raging debates. "We established an ongoing series of general manager meetings, and my role was more as a mediator," commented Iverson. "They were chaos. We would stay there for hours, ironing out the issues, until we came to something....At times, the meetings would get so violent that people almost went across the table at each other....People yelled. They waved their arms around and pounded on tables. Faces would get red and veins bulged out."[38]

Iverson's assistant tells of a scene repeated over the years, wherein colleagues would march into Iverson's office and yell and scream at each other, but then emerge with a conclusion.[39] Argue and debate, then sell the nuclear business; argue and debate, then focus on steel joists; argue and debate, then begin to manufacture their own steel; argue and debate, then invest in their own mini-mill; argue and debate, then build a second mini-mill, and so forth. Nearly all the Nucor executives we spoke with described a climate of debate, wherein the company's strategy "evolved through many agonizing arguments and fights."[40]

> Like Nucor, all the good-to-great companies had a penchant for intense dialogue. Phrases like "loud debate," "heated discussions," and "healthy conflict" peppered the articles and interview transcripts from all the companies. They didn't use discussion as a sham process to let people "have their say" so that they could "buy in" to a predetermined decision. The process was more like a heated scientific debate, with people engaged in a search for the best answers.

3. Conduct autopsies, without blame.

In 1978, Philip Morris acquired the Seven-Up Company, only to sell it eight years later at a loss.[41] The financial loss was relatively small compared to Philip Morris's total assets, but it was a highly visible black eye that consumed thousands of hours of precious management time.

In our interviews with the Philip Morris executives, we were struck by how they all brought up the debacle on their own and discussed it openly. Instead of hiding their big, ugly mistake, they seemed to feel an almost therapeutic need to talk about it. In his book, *I'm a Lucky Guy*, Joe Cullman dedicates five pages to dissecting the 7UP disaster. He doesn't hold back the embarrassing truth about how flawed the decision was. It is a five-page clinical analysis of the mistake, its implications, and its lessons.

Hundreds, if not thousands, of people hours had been spent in autopsies of the 7UP case. Yet, as much as they talked about this conspicuous failure, no one pointed fingers to single out blame. There is only one exception to this pattern: Joe Cullman, standing in front of the mirror, pointing the finger right at himself. "[It]... became apparent that this was another Joe Cullman plan that didn't work," he writes.[42] He goes even further, implying that if he'd only listened better to the people who challenged his idea at the time, the disaster might have been averted. He goes out of his way to give credit to those who were right in retrospect, naming those specific individuals who were more prescient than himself.

In an era when leaders go to great lengths to preserve the image of their own track record—stepping forth to claim credit about how they were visionary when their colleagues were not, but finding others to blame when their decisions go awry—it is quite refreshing to come across Cullman. He set the tone: "I will take responsibility for this bad decision. But we will all take responsibility for extracting the maximum learning from the tuition we've paid."

> When you conduct autopsies without blame, you go a long way toward creating a climate where the truth is heard. If you have the right people on the bus, you should almost never need to assign blame but need only to search for understanding and learning.

4. Build "red flag" mechanisms.
We live in an information age, when those with more and better information supposedly have an advantage. If you look across the rise and fall of organizations, however, you will rarely find companies stumbling because they lacked information.

Bethlehem Steel executives had known for years about the threat of mini-mill companies like Nucor. They paid little attention until they woke up one day to discover large chunks of market share taken away.[43]

Upjohn had plenty of information that indicated some of its forthcoming products would fail to deliver anticipated results or, worse, had potentially serious side effects. Yet it often ignored those problems. With Halcion, for example, an insider was quoted in *Newsweek* saying, "dismissing safety concerns about Halcion had become virtual company policy." In another case when Upjohn found itself under fire, it framed its problems as "adverse publicity," rather than confronting the truth of its own shortcomings.[44]

Executives at Bank of America had plenty of information about the realities of deregulation, yet they failed to confront the one big implication of those realities: In a deregulated world, banking would be a commodity, and the old perks and genteel traditions of banking would be gone forever. Not until it had lost $1.8 billion did Bank of America fully accept this fact. In contrast, Carl Reichardt of Wells Fargo, called the ultimate realist by his predecessor, hit the brutal facts of deregulation head-on.[45] Sorry, fellow bankers, but we can preserve the banker class no more. We've got to be businessmen with as much attention to costs and effectiveness as McDonald's.

> Indeed, we found no evidence that the good-to-great companies had more or better information than the comparison companies. None. Both sets of companies had virtually identical access to good information. The key, then, lies not in better information, but in turning information into information *that cannot be ignored*.

One particularly powerful way to accomplish this is through red flag mechanisms. Allow me to use a personal example to illustrate the idea. When teaching by the case method at Stanford Business School, I issued to each MBA student an 8.5" × 11" bright red sheet of paper, with the following instructions:

"This is your red flag for the quarter. If you raise your hand with your red flag, the classroom will stop for you. There are no restrictions on when and how to use your red flag; the decision rests entirely in your hands. You can use it to voice an observation, share a personal experience, present an analysis, disagree with the professor, challenge a CEO guest, respond to a fellow student, ask a question, make a suggestion, or whatever. There will be no penalty whatsoever for any use of a red flag. Your red flag can be used only once during the quarter. Your red flag is nontransferable; you cannot give or sell it to another student."

With the red flag, I had no idea precisely *what* would happen each day in class. In one situation, a student used her red flag to state, "Professor Collins, I think you are doing a particularly ineffective job of running class today. You are leading too much with your questions and stifling our independent thinking. Let us think for ourselves." The red flag confronted me with the brutal fact that my own questioning style stood in the way of people's learning. A student survey at the end of the quarter would have given me that same information. But the red flag—real time, in front of everyone in the classroom—turned information about the shortcomings of the class into information that I absolutely could not ignore.

I got the idea for red flag mechanisms from Bruce Woolpert, who instituted a particularly powerful device called short pay at his company Graniterock. Short pay gives the customer full discretionary power to decide whether and how much to pay on an invoice based upon his own subjective evaluation of how satisfied he feels with a product or service. Short pay is not a refund policy. The customer does not need to return the product, nor does he need to call Graniterock for permission. He simply circles the offending item on the invoice, deducts it from the total, and sends a check for the balance. When I asked Woolpert his reasons for short pay, he said, "You can get a lot of information from customer surveys, but there are always ways of explaining away the data. With short pay, you absolutely have to pay attention to the data. You often don't know that a customer is upset until you lose that customer entirely. Short pay acts as an early warning system that forces us to adjust quickly, long before we would lose that customer."

To be clear, we did not generally find red flag mechanisms as vivid and dramatic as short pay in the good-to-great companies. Nonetheless, I've decided to include this idea here, at the urging of research assistant Lane Hornung. Hornung, who helped me systematically research and collate mechanisms across companies for a different research project, makes the compelling argument that if you're a fully developed Level 5 leader, you might not need red flag mechanisms. But if you are not yet a Level 5 leader, or if you suffer the liability of charisma, red flag mechanisms give you a practical and useful tool for turning information into information that cannot be ignored and for creating a climate where the truth is heard.*

UNWAVERING FAITH AMID THE BRUTAL FACTS

When Procter & Gamble invaded the paper-based consumer business in the late 1960s, Scott Paper (then the leader) simply resigned itself to second place without a fight and began looking for ways to diversify.[46] "The company had a meeting for analysts in 1971 that was one of the most depressing I've ever attended," said one analyst. "Management essentially threw in the towel and said, 'We've been had.' "[47] The once-proud company began to look at its competition and say, "Here's how we stack up against the best," and sigh, "Oh, well ... at least there are people in the business worse than we are."[48] Instead of figuring out how to get back on the offensive and win, Scott just tried to protect what it had. Conceding the top end of the market to P&G, Scott hoped that, by hiding away in the B category, it would be left alone by the big monster that had invaded its turf.[49]

Kimberly-Clark, on the other hand, viewed competing against Procter & Gamble not as a liability, but as an *asset*. Darwin Smith and his team felt exhilarated by the idea of going up against the best, seeing it as an opportunity to make Kimberly-Clark better and stronger. They also viewed it as a way to stimulate the competitive juices of Kimberly people at all levels. At one internal gathering, Darwin Smith stood up and started his talk by saying, "Okay, I want everyone to rise in a moment of silence." Everyone looked around, wondering what Darwin was up to. Did someone die? And so, after a moment of confusion, they all stood up and stared at their shoes in reverent silence. After an appropriate pause, Smith looked out at the group and said in a somber tone, "That was a moment of silence for P&G."

The place went bananas. Blair White, a director who witnessed the incident, said, "He had everyone wound up in this thing, all up and down the company, right down to the plant floor. We were taking on Goliath!"[50] Later, Wayne Sanders (Smith's successor) described to us the incredible benefit of competing against the best: "Could we have a better adversary than P&G? Not a chance. I say that because we respect them so much. They are bigger than we are. They are very talented. They are great at marketing. They beat the hell out of every one of their competitors, except one, Kimberly-Clark. That is one of the things that makes us so proud."[51]

Scott Paper's and Kimberly-Clark's differing reactions to P&G bring us to a vital point. In confronting the brutal facts, the good-to-great companies left themselves stronger and more resilient, not weaker and more dispirited. There is a sense of exhilaration that comes in facing head-on the hard truths and saying, "We will never give up. We will never capitulate. It might take a long time, but we *will* find a way to prevail."

Robert Aders of Kroger summed this up nicely at the end of his interview, describing the psychology of the Kroger team as it faced the daunting twenty-year task of methodically turning over the entire Kroger system. "There was a certain Churchillian character to what we were doing. We had a very strong will to live, the sense that we are Kroger, Kroger was here before and will be here long after we are gone, and, by god, we are going to win this thing. *It might take us a hundred years, but we will persist for a hundred years, if that's what it takes.*"[52]

Throughout our research, we were continually reminded of the "hardiness" research studies done by the International Committee for the Study of Victimization. These studies looked at people who had suffered serious adversity —cancer patients, prisoners of war, accident victims, and so forth—and survived. They found that people fell generally into three categories: those who were permanently dispirited by the event, those who got their life back to normal, and those who used the experience as a defining event that made them stronger.[53] The good-to-great companies were like those in the third group, with the "hardiness factor."

When Fannie Mae began its transition in the early 1980s, almost no one gave it high odds for success, much less for greatness. Fannie Mae had $56 billion of loans that were losing money. It received about 9 percent interest on its mortgage portfolio but had to pay up to 15 percent on the debt it issued. Multiply that difference times $56 billion, and you get a very large negative number! Furthermore, by charter, Fannie Mae could not diversify outside the mortgage finance business. Most people viewed Fannie Mae as totally beholden to shifts in the direction of interest rates—they go up and Fannie Mae loses, they go down and Fannie Mae wins—and many believed that Fannie Mae could succeed only if the government stepped in to clamp down on interest rates.[54] "That's their only hope," said one analyst.[55]

But that's not the way David Maxwell and his newly assembled team viewed the situation. They never wavered in their faith, consistently emphasizing in their interviews with us that they never had the goal to merely survive but to *prevail* in the end as a great company. Yes, the interest spread was a brutal fact that was not going to magically disappear. Fannie Mae had no choice but to become the best capital markets player in the world at managing mortgage interest risk. Maxwell and his team set out to create a new business model that would depend much less on interest rates, involving the invention of very sophisticated mortgage finance instruments. Most analysts responded with derision. "When you've got $56 billion worth of loans in place and underwater, talking about new programs is a joke," said one. "That's like Chrysler [then asking for federal loan guarantees to stave off bankruptcy] going into the aircraft business."[56]

After completing my interview with David Maxwell, I asked how he and his team dealt with the naysayers during those dark days. "It was never an issue internally," he said. "Of course, we had to stop doing a lot of stupid things, and we had to invent a completely new set of financial devices. But we never entertained the possibility that we would fail. We were going to use the calamity as an opportunity to remake Fannie Mae into a great company."[57]

During a research meeting, a team member commented that Fannie Mae reminded her of an old television show, *The Six Million Dollar Man* with Lee Majors. The pretext of the series is that an astronaut suffers a serious crash while testing a moon landing craft over a southwestern desert. Instead of just trying to save the patient, doctors completely redesign him into a superhuman cyborg, installing atomic-powered robotic devices such as a powerful left eye and mechanical limbs.[58] Similarly, David Maxwell and his team didn't use the fact that Fannie Mae was bleeding and near death as a pretext to merely restructure the company. They used it as an opportunity to create something much stronger and more powerful. Step by step, day by day, month by month, the Fannie Mae team rebuilt the entire business model around risk management and reshaped the corporate culture into a high-performance machine that rivaled anything on Wall Street, eventually generating stock returns nearly eight times the market over fifteen years.

THE STOCKDALE PARADOX

Of course, not all good-to-great companies faced a dire crisis like Fannie Mae; fewer than half did. But every good-to-great company faced significant adversity along the way to greatness, of one sort or another—Gillette and the takeover battles, Nucor and imports, Wells Fargo and deregulation, Pitney Bowes losing its monopoly, Abbott Labs and a huge product recall, Kroger and the need to replace nearly 100 percent of its stores, and so forth. In every case, the management team responded with a powerful psychological duality. On the one hand, they stoically accepted the brutal facts of reality. On the other hand, they maintained an unwavering faith in the endgame, and a commitment to prevail as a great company despite the brutal facts. We came to call this duality the Stockdale Paradox.

The name refers to Admiral Jim Stockdale, who was the highest-ranking United States military officer in the "Hanoi Hilton" prisoner-of-war camp during the height of the Vietnam War. Tortured over twenty times during his eight-year imprisonment from 1965 to 1973, Stockdale lived out the war without any prisoner's rights, no set release date, and no certainty as to whether he would even survive to see his family again. He shouldered the burden of command, doing everything he could to create conditions that would increase the number of prisoners who would survive unbroken, while fighting an internal war against his captors and their attempts to use the prisoners for propaganda. At one point, he beat himself with a stool and cut himself with a razor, deliberately disfiguring himself, so that he could not be put on videotape as an example of a "well-treated prisoner." He exchanged secret intelligence information with his wife through their letters, knowing that discovery would mean more torture and perhaps death. He instituted rules that would help people to deal with torture (no one can resist torture indefinitely, so he created a stepwise system—after x minutes, you can say certain things—that gave the men milestones to survive toward). He instituted an elaborate internal communications system to reduce the sense of isolation that their captors tried to create, which used a five-by-five matrix of tap codes for alpha characters. (Tap-tap equals the letter a, tap-pause-tap-tap equals the letter b, tap-tap-pause-tap equals the letter f, and so forth, for twenty-five letters, c doubling in for k.) At one point, during an imposed silence, the prisoners mopped and swept the central yard using the code, swish-swashing out "We love you" to Stockdale, on the third anniversary of his being shot down. After his release, Stockdale became the first three-star officer in the history of the navy to wear both aviator wings and the Congressional Medal of Honor.[59]

You can understand, then, my anticipation at the prospect of spending part of an afternoon with Stockdale. One of my students had written his paper on Stockdale, who happened to be a senior research fellow studying the Stoic philosophers at the Hoover Institution right across the street from my office, and Stockdale invited the two of us for lunch. In preparation, I read *In Love and War*, the book Stockdale and his wife had written in alternating chapters, chronicling their experiences during those eight years.

As I moved through the book, I found myself getting depressed. It just seemed so bleak—the uncertainty of his fate, the brutality of his captors, and so forth. And then, it dawned on me: "Here I am sitting in my warm and comfortable office, looking out over the beautiful Stanford campus on a beautiful Saturday afternoon. I'm getting depressed reading this, and I know the end of the story! I know that he gets out, reunites with his family, becomes a national hero, and gets to spend the later years of his life studying philosophy on this same beautiful campus. If it feels depressing for me, how on earth did he deal with it when he was actually there and *did not know the end of the story?*"

"I never lost faith in the end of the story," he said, when I asked him. "I never doubted not only that I would get out, but also that I would prevail in the end and turn the experience into the defining event of my life, which, in retrospect, I would not trade."

*

I didn't say anything for many minutes, and we continued the slow walk toward the faculty club, Stockdale limping and arc-swinging his stiff leg that had never fully recovered from repeated torture. Finally, after about a hundred meters of silence, I asked, "Who didn't make it out?"

"Oh, that's easy," he said. "The optimists."

"The optimists? I don't understand," I said, now completely confused, given what he'd said a hundred meters earlier.

"The optimists. Oh, they were the ones who said, 'We're going to be out by Christmas.' And Christmas would come, and Christmas would go. Then they'd say, 'We're going to be out by Easter.' And Easter would come, and Easter would go. And then Thanksgiving, and then it would be Christmas again. And they died of a broken heart."

Another long pause, and more walking. Then he turned to me and said, "This is a very important lesson. You must never confuse faith that you will prevail in the end—which you can never afford to lose—with the discipline to confront the most brutal facts of your current reality, whatever they might be."

To this day, I carry a mental image of Stockdale admonishing the optimists: "We're not getting out by Christmas; deal with it!"

*

That conversation with Admiral Stockdale stayed with me, and in fact had a profound influence on my own development. Life is unfair—sometimes to our advantage, sometimes to our disadvantage. We will all experience disappointments and crushing events somewhere along the way, setbacks for which there is no "reason," no one to blame. It might be disease; it might be injury; it might be an accident; it might be losing a loved one; it might be getting swept away in a political shake-up; it might be getting shot down over Vietnam and thrown into a POW camp for eight years. What separates people, Stockdale taught me, is not the presence or absence of difficulty, but how they deal with the inevitable difficulties of life. In wrestling with life's challenges, the Stockdale Paradox (you must retain faith that you will prevail in the end and you must also confront the most brutal facts of your current reality) has proved powerful for coming back from difficulties not weakened, but stronger—not just for me, but for all those who've learned the lesson and tried to apply it.

The Stockdale Paradox

| Retain faith that you will prevail in the end, regardless of the difficulties. | *AND at the same time* | Confront the most brutal facts of your current reality, whatever they might be. |

I never really considered my walk with Stockdale as part of my research into great companies, categorizing it more as a personal rather than corporate lesson. But as we unraveled the research evidence, I kept coming back to it in my own mind. Finally, one day during a research-team meeting, I shared the Stockdale story. There was silence around the table when I finished, and I thought, "They must think I'm really out in left field."

Then Duane Duffy, a quiet and thoughtful team member who had done the A&P versus Kroger analysis, said, "That's exactly what I've been struggling with. I've been trying to get my hands around the essential difference between A&P and Kroger. And that's it. Kroger was like Stockdale, and A&P was like the optimists who always thought they'd be out by Christmas."

Then other team members began to chime in, noting the same difference between their comparison sets—Wells Fargo versus Bank of America both facing deregulation, Kimberly-Clark versus Scott Paper both facing the terrible might of Procter & Gamble, Pitney Bowes versus Addressograph both facing the loss of their monopolies, Nucor versus Bethlehem Steel both facing imports, and so forth. They all demonstrated this paradoxical psychological pattern, and we dubbed it the Stockdale Paradox.

The Stockdale Paradox is a signature of all those who create greatness, be it in leading their own lives or in leading others. Churchill had it during the Second World War. Admiral Stockdale, like Viktor Frankl before him, lived it in a prison camp. And while our good-to-great companies cannot claim to have experienced either the grandeur of saving the free world or the depth of personal experience of living in a POW camp, they all embraced the Stockdale Paradox. It didn't matter how bleak the situation or how stultifying their mediocrity, they all maintained unwavering faith that they would not just survive, but prevail as a great company. And yet, at the same time, they became relentlessly disciplined at confronting the most brutal facts of their current reality.

Like much of what we found in our research, the key elements of greatness are deceptively simple and straightforward. The good-to-great leaders were able to strip away so much noise and clutter and just focus on the few things that would have the greatest impact. They were able to do so in large part because they operated from both sides of the Stockdale Paradox, never letting one side overshadow the other. If you are able to adopt this dual pattern, you will dramatically increase the odds of making a series of good decisions and ultimately discovering a simple, yet deeply insightful, concept for making the really big choices. And once you have that simple, unifying concept, you will be very close to making a sustained transition to breakthrough results. It is to the creation of that concept that we now turn.

---

*Keep in mind, this was the early 1970s, a full decade before the "number one, number two, or exit" idea became mainstream. Kroger, like all good-to-great companies, developed its ideas by paying attention to the data right in front of it, not by following trends and fads set by others. Interestingly, over half the good-to-great companies had some version of the "number one, number two" concept in place years before it became a management fad.

*For a more complete discussion of mechanisms, see the article "Turning Goals into Results: The Power of

Catalytic Mechanisms," *Harvard Business Review*, July–August, 1999.

Chapter Summary
Confront The Brutal Facts
(Yet Never Lose Faith)

KEY POINTS

• All good-to-great companies began the process of finding a path to greatness by confronting the brutal facts of their current reality.

• When you start with an honest and diligent effort to determine the truth of your situation, the right decisions often become self-evident. It is impossible to make good decisions without infusing the entire process with an honest confrontation of the brutal facts.

• A primary task in taking a company from good to great is to create a culture wherein people have a tremendous opportunity to be heard and, ultimately, for the truth to be heard.

• Creating a climate where the truth is heard involves four basic practices:

    1. Lead with questions, not answers.
    2. Engage in dialogue and debate, not coercion.
    3. Conduct autopsies, without blame.
    4. Build red flag mechanisms that turn information into information that cannot be ignored.

• The good-to-great companies faced just as much adversity as the comparison companies, but responded to that adversity differently. They hit the realities of their situation head-on. As a result, they emerged from adversity even stronger.

• A key psychology for leading from good to great is the Stockdale

Paradox: Retain absolute faith that you can and will prevail in the end, regardless of the difficulties, *AND at the same time* confront the most brutal facts of your current reality, whatever they might be.

UNEXPECTED FINDINGS

• Charisma can be as much a liability as an asset, as the strength of your leadership personality can deter people from bringing you the brutal facts.

• Leadership does not begin just with vision. It begins with getting people to confront the brutal facts and to act on the implications.

• Spending time and energy trying to "motivate" people is a waste of effort. The real question is not, "How do we motivate our people?" If you have the right people, they will be self-motivated. The key is to not *de*-motivate them. One of the primary ways to de-motivate people is to ignore the brutal facts of reality.

CHAPTER 5
The Hedgehog Concept
Simplicty within the Three Circles

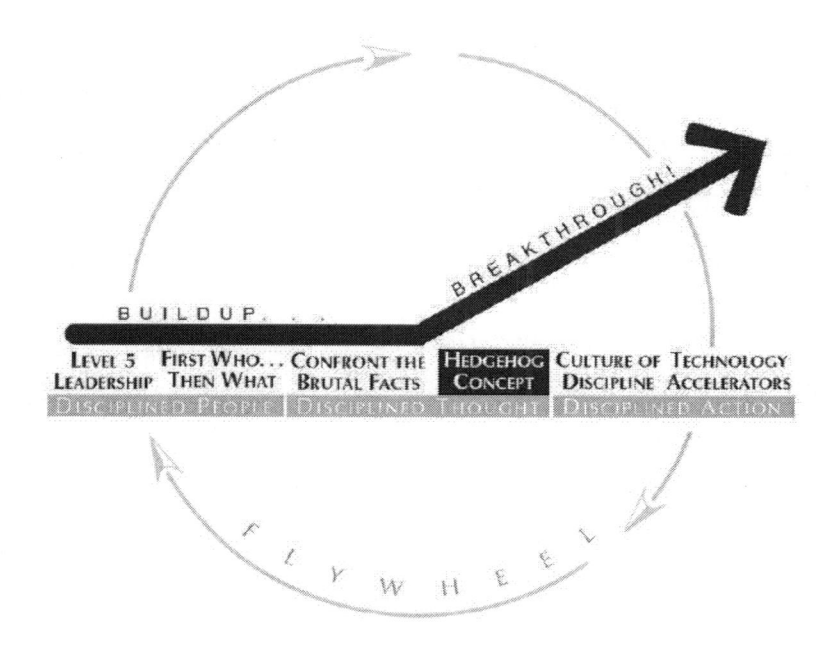

> Know thyself.
>
> —Scribes of Delphi,
> via Plato[1]

Are you a hedgehog or a fox?

In his famous essay "The Hedgehog and the Fox," Isaiah Berlin divided the world into hedgehogs and foxes, based upon an ancient Greek parable: "The fox knows many things, but the hedgehog knows one big thing."[2] The fox is a cunning creature, able to devise a myriad of complex strategies for sneak attacks upon the hedgehog. Day in and day out, the fox circles around the hedgehog's den, waiting for the perfect moment to pounce. Fast, sleek, beautiful, fleet of foot, and crafty—the fox looks like the sure winner. The hedgehog, on the other hand, is a dowdier creature, looking like a genetic mix-up between a porcupine and a small armadillo. He waddles along, going about his simple day, searching for lunch and taking care of his home.

The fox waits in cunning silence at the juncture in the trail. The hedgehog, minding his own business, wanders right into the path of the fox. "Aha, I've got you now!" thinks the fox. He leaps out, bounding across the ground, lightning fast. The little hedgehog, sensing danger, looks up and thinks, "Here we go again. Will he ever learn?" Rolling up into a perfect little ball, the hedgehog becomes a sphere of sharp spikes, pointing outward in all directions. The fox, bounding toward his prey, sees the hedgehog defense and calls off the attack. Retreating back to the forest, the fox begins to calculate a new line of attack. Each day, some version of this battle between the hedgehog and the fox takes place, and despite the greater cunning of the fox, the hedgehog always wins.

Berlin extrapolated from this little parable to divide people into two basic groups: foxes and hedgehogs. Foxes pursue many ends at the same time and see the world in all its complexity. They are "scattered or diffused, moving on many levels," says Berlin, never integrating their thinking into one overall concept or unifying vision. Hedgehogs, on the other hand, simplify a complex world into a single organizing idea, a basic principle or concept that unifies and guides everything. It doesn't matter how complex the world, a hedgehog reduces all challenges and dilemmas to simple— indeed almost simplistic—hedgehog ideas. For a hedgehog, anything that does not somehow relate to the hedgehog idea holds no relevance.

Princeton professor Marvin Bressler pointed out the power of the hedgehog during one of our long conversations: "You want to know what separates those who make the biggest impact from all the others who are just as smart? They're hedgehogs." Freud and the unconscious, Darwin and natural selection, Marx and class struggle, Einstein and relativity, Adam Smith and division of labor—they were all hedgehogs. They took a complex world and simplified it. "Those who leave the biggest footprints," said Bressler, "have thousands calling after them, 'Good idea, but you went too far!' "[3]

To be clear, hedgehogs are not stupid. Quite the contrary. They understand that the essence of profound insight is simplicity. What could be more simple than $e = mc^2$? What could be simpler than the idea of the unconscious, organized into an id, ego, and superego? What could be more elegant than Adam Smith's pin factory and "invisible hand"? No, the hedgehogs aren't simpletons; they have a piercing insight that allows them to see through complexity and discern underlying patterns. Hedgehogs see what is essential, and ignore the rest.

What does all this talk of hedgehogs and foxes have to do with good to great?

Everything.

> Those who built the good-to-great companies were, to one degree or another, hedgehogs. They used their hedgehog nature to drive toward what we came to call a Hedgehog Concept for their companies. Those who led the comparison companies tended to be foxes, never gaining the clarifying advantage of a Hedgehog Concept, being instead scattered, diffused, and inconsistent.

Consider the case of Walgreens versus Eckerd. Recall how Walgreens generated cumulative stock returns from the end of 1975 to 2000 that exceeded the market by over fifteen times, handily beating such great companies as GE, Merck, Coca-Cola, and Intel. It was a remarkable performance for such an anonymous —some might even say boring—company. When interviewing Cork Walgreen, I kept asking him to go deeper, to help us understand these extraordinary results. Finally, in exasperation, he said, "Look, it just wasn't that complicated! Once we understood the concept, we just moved straight ahead."[4]

What was the concept? Simply this: the best, most convenient drugstores, with high profit per customer visit. That's it. That's the breakthrough strategy that Walgreens used to beat Intel, GE, Coca-Cola, and Merck.

In classic hedgehog style, Walgreens took this simple concept and implemented it with fanatical consistency. It embarked on a systematic program to replace all inconvenient locations with more convenient ones, preferably corner lots where customers could easily enter and exit from multiple directions. If a great corner location would open up just half a block away from a profitable Walgreens store in a good location, the company would close the good store (even at a cost of $1 million to get out of the lease) to open a great new store on the corner.[5] Walgreens pioneered drive-through pharmacies, found customers liked the idea, and built hundreds of them. In urban areas, the company clustered its stores tightly together, on the precept that no one should have to walk more than a few blocks to reach a Walgreens.[6] In downtown San Francisco, for example, Walgreens clustered nine stores within a one-mile radius. Nine stores![7] If you look closely, you will see Walgreens stores as densely packed in some cities as Starbucks coffee shops in Seattle.

Walgreens then linked its convenience concept to a simple economic idea, profit per customer visit. Tight clustering (nine stores per mile!) leads to local economies of scale, which provides the cash for more clustering, which in turn draws more customers. By adding high-margin services, like one-hour photo developing, Walgreens increased its profit per customer visit. More convenience led to more customer visits, which, when multiplied times increased profit per customer visit, threw cash back into the system to build *even more* convenient stores. Store by store, block by block, city by city, region by region, Walgreens became more and more of a hedgehog with this incredibly simple idea.

WALGREENS VERSUS SELECTED GREAT COMPANIES
Cumulative Stock Returns of $1 Invested,
December 31, 1975 – January 1, 2000

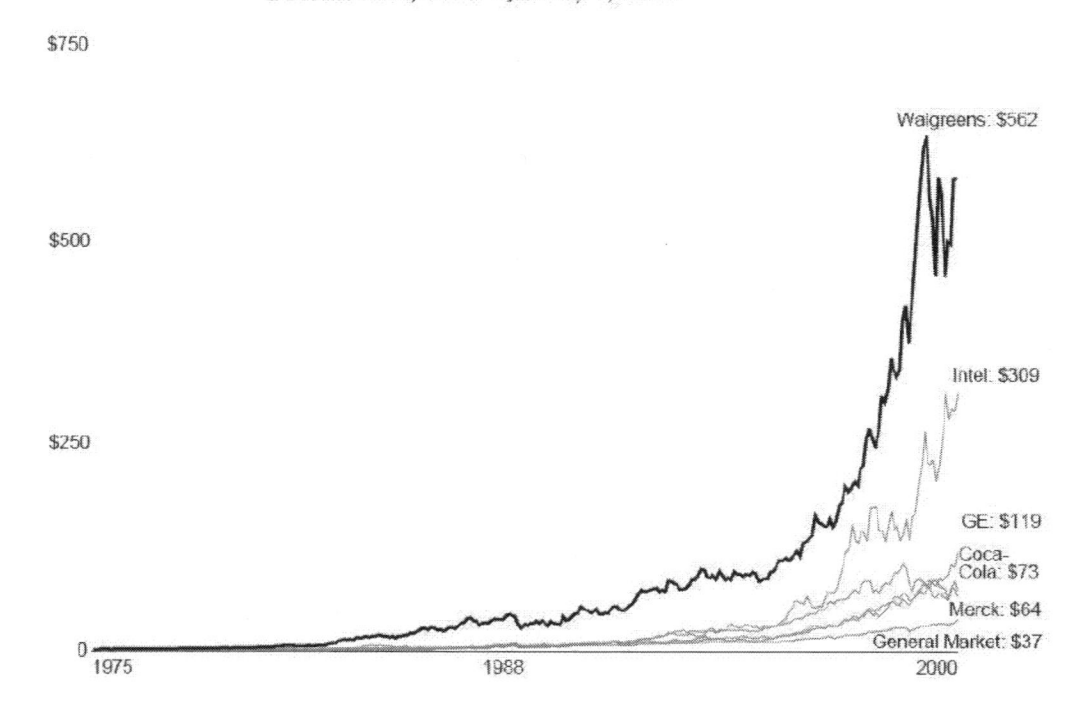

- Walgreens: $562
- Intel: $309
- GE: $119
- Coca-Cola: $73
- Merck: $64
- General Market: $37

In a world overrun by management faddists, brilliant visionaries, ranting futurists, fearmongers, motivational gurus, and all the rest, it's refreshing to see a company succeed so brilliantly by taking one simple concept and just doing it with excellence and imagination. Becoming the best in the world at convenient drugstores, steadily increasing profit per customer visit—what could be more obvious and straightforward?

Yet, if it was so obvious and straightforward, why didn't Eckerd see it? While Walgreens stuck *only* to cities where it could implement the convenience/clustering concept, we found no evidence of a similarly coherent concept for growth at Eckerd. Deal makers to the core, Eckerd's executives compulsively leapt at opportunities to acquire clumps of stores—forty-two units here, thirty-six units there—in hodgepodge fashion, with no obvious unifying theme.

While Walgreens executives understood that profitable growth would come by pruning away all that did not fit with the Hedgehog Concept, Eckerd executives lurched after growth for growth's sake. In the early 1980s, just as Walgreens became religious about carrying out its convenient drugstore concept, Eckerd threw itself into the home video market with its purchase of American Home Video Corporation. Eckerd's CEO told *Forbes* magazine in 1981, "Some feel the purer we are the better we'll be. But I want growth, and the home video industry is only emerging— unlike, say, drugstore chains."[8] Eckerd's home video foray produced $31 million in losses before Eckerd sold it to Tandy, which crowed that it got the deal for $72 million below book value.[9]

In the precise year of Eckerd's American Home Video acquisition, Walgreens and Eckerd had virtually identical revenues ($1.7 billion). Ten years later, Walgreens had grown to over twice the revenues of Eckerd, accumulating net profits $1 billion greater than Eckerd over the decade. Twenty years later, Walgreens was going strong, as one of the most sustained transformations in our study. Meanwhile, Eckerd ceased to exist as an independent company.[10]

Made in the USA
Columbia, SC
28 August 2024